MAXIM

FIRE APPARATUS
PHOTO HISTORY

Howard T. Smith

Iconografix
Photo History Series

Iconografix
PO Box 446
Hudson, Wisconsin 54016 USA

Library of Congress Control Number: 2003115055

ISBN 1-58388-111-5

04 05 06 07 08 09 5 4 3 2 1

Printed in China

Cover and book design by Dan Perry

Copyedited by Suzie Helberg

Cover Photo: Canterbury, Connecticut owned this
1984 Maxim "S" model with 1,000-gpm pump and
large 1200-gallon water tank. *Photo by Mark Redman,
from collection of Charlie Beckwith*

BOOK PROPOSALS

Iconografix is a publishing company
specializing in books for transportation enthusiasts. We publish in a
number of different areas, including
Automobiles, Auto Racing, Buses,
Construction Equipment, Emergency
Equipment, Farming Equipment, Rail-
roads & Trucks. The Iconografix imprint
is constantly growing and expanding
into new subject areas.

Authors, editors, and knowledgeable
enthusiasts in the field of transportation history are invited to contact
the Editorial Department at Iconografix,
Inc., PO Box 446, Hudson, WI 54016.

More Great Titles From **Iconografix**

EMERGENCY VEHICLES

The American Ambulance 1900-2002: An Illustrated History ISBN 1-58388-081-X
American Funeral Vehicles 1883-2003 Illustrated History ISBN 1-58388-104-2
American LaFrance 700 Series 1945-1952 Photo Archive ISBN 1-882256-90-5
American LaFrance 700 Series 1945-1952 Photo Archive Volume 2 ISBN 1-58388-025-9
American LaFrance 700 & 800 Series 1953-1958 Photo Archive ISBN 1-882256-91-3
American LaFrance 900 Series 1958-1964 Photo Archive ISBN 1-58388-002-X
Classic Seagrave 1935-1951 Photo Archive ISBN 1-58388-034-8
Crown Firecoach 1951-1985 Photo Archive ISBN 1-58388-047-X
Encyclopedia of Canadian Fire Apparatus ISBN 1-58388-119-0
Fire Chief Cars 1900-1997 Photo Album ISBN 1-882256-87-5
Hahn Fire Apparatus 1923-1990 Photo Archive ISBN 1-58388-077-1
Heavy Rescue Trucks 1931-2000 Photo Gallery ISBN 1-58388-045-3
Imperial Fire Apparatus 1969-1976 Photo Archive ISBN 1-58388-091-7
Industrial and Private Fire Apparatus 1925-2001 Photo Archive ISBN 1-58388-049-6
*Mack Model C Fire Trucks 1957-1967 Photo Archive** ISBN 1-58388-014-3
*Mack Model L Fire Trucks 1940-1954 Photo Archive** ISBN 1-882256-86-7
Maxim Fire Apparatus 1914-1989 Photo Archive ISBN 1-58388-050-X
Maxim Fire Apparatus Photo History ISBN 1-58388-111-5
Navy & Marine Corps Fire Apparatus 1836 -2000 Photo Gallery ISBN 1-58388-031-3
Pierre Thibault Ltd. Fire Apparatus 1918-1990 Photo Archive ISBN 1-58388-074-7
Pirsch Fire Apparatus 1890-1991 Photo Archive ISBN 1-58388-082-8
Police Cars: Restoring, Collecting & Showing America's Finest Sedans ISBN 1-58388-046-1
Saulsbury Fire Rescue Apparatus 1956-2003 Photo Archive ISBN 1-58388-106-9
Seagrave 70th Anniversary Series Photo Archive ISBN 1-58388-001-1
TASC Fire Apparatus 1946-1985 Photo Archive ISBN 1-58388-065-8
Volunteer & Rural Fire Apparatus Photo Gallery ISBN 1-58388-005-4
W.S. Darley & Co. Fire Apparatus 1908-2000 Photo Archive ISBN 1-58388-061-5
Wildland Fire Apparatus 1940-2001 Photo Gallery ISBN 1-58388-056-9
Young Fire Equipment 1932-1991 Photo Archive ISBN 1-58388-015-1

TRUCKS

Autocar Trucks 1899-1950 Photo Archive ISBN 1-58388-115-8
Autocar Trucks 1950-1987 Photo Archive ISBN 1-58388-072-0
Beverage Trucks 1910-1975 Photo Archive ISBN 1-882256-60-3
*Brockway Trucks 1948-1961 Photo Archive** ISBN 1-882256-55-7
Chevrolet El Camino Photo History Incl. GMC Sprint & Caballero ISBN 1-58388-044-5
Circus and Carnival Trucks 1923-2000 Photo Archive ISBN 1-58388-048-8
Dodge B-Series Trucks Restorer's & Collector's Reference Guide and History ISBN 1-58388-087-9
Dodge Pickups 1939-1978 Photo Album ISBN 1-882256-82-4
Dodge Power Wagons 1940-1980 Photo Archive ISBN 1-882256-89-1
Dodge Power Wagon Photo History ISBN 1-58388-019-4
Dodge Ram Trucks 1994-2001 Photo History ISBN 1-58388-051-8
Dodge Trucks 1929-1947 Photo Archive ISBN 1-882256-36-0
Dodge Trucks 1948-1960 Photo Archive ISBN 1-882256-37-9
Ford 4x4s 1935-1990 Photo History ISBN 1-58388-079-8
Ford Heavy-Duty Trucks 1948-1998 Photo History ISBN 1-58388-043-7
Freightliner Trucks 1937-1981 Photo Archive ISBN 1-58388-090-9
Jeep 1941-2000 Photo Archive ISBN 1-58388-021-6
Jeep Prototypes & Concept Vehicles Photo Archive ISBN 1-58388-033-X
*Mack Model AB Photo Archive** ISBN 1-882256-18-2
*Mack AP Super-Duty Trucks 1926-1938 Photo Archive** ISBN 1-882256-54-9
*Mack Model B 1953-1966 Volume 2 Photo Archive** ISBN 1-882256-34-4
*Mack EB-EC-ED-EE-EF-EG-DE 1936-1951 Photo Archive** ISBN 1-882256-29-8
*Mack EH-EJ-EM-EQ-ER-ES 1936-1950 Photo Archive** ISBN 1-882256-39-5
*Mack FC-FCSW-NW 1936-1947 Photo Archive** ISBN 1-882256-28-X
*Mack FG-FH-FJ-FK-FN-FP-FT-FW 1937-1950 Photo Archive** ISBN 1-882256-35-2
*Mack LF-LH-LJ-LM-LT 1940-1956 Photo Archive** ISBN 1-882256-38-7
*Mack Trucks Photo Gallery** ISBN 1-882256-88-3
New Car Carriers 1910-1998 Photo Album ISBN 1-882256-98-0
Plymouth Commercial Vehicles Photo Archive ISBN 1-58388-004-6
Refuse Trucks Photo Archive ISBN 1-58388-042-9
Studebaker Trucks 1927-1940 Photo Archive ISBN 1-882256-40-9
White Trucks 1900-1937 Photo Archive ISBN 1-882256-80-8

BUSES

Buses of ACF Photo Archive Including ACF-Brill And CCF-Brill ISBN 1-58388-101-8
Buses of Motor Coach Industries 1932-2000 Photo Archive ISBN 1-58388-039-9
Fageol & Twin Coach Buses 1922-1956 Photo Archive ISBN 1-58388-075-5
Flxible Intercity Buses 1924-1970 Photo Archive ISBN 1-58388-108-5
Flxible Transit Buses 1953-1995 Photo Archive ISBN 1-58388-053-4
GM Intercity Coaches 1944-1980 Photo Archive ISBN 1-58388-099-2
Greyhound Buses 1914-2000 Photo Archive ISBN 1-58388-027-5
*Mack® Buses 1900-1960 Photo Archive** ISBN 1-58388-020-8
Prevost Buses 1924-2002 Photo Archive ISBN 1-58388-083-6
Trailways Buses 1936-2001 Photo Archive ISBN 1-58388-029-1
Trolley Buses 1913-2001 Photo Archive ISBN 1-58388-057-7
Yellow Coach Buses 1923-1943 Photo Archive ISBN 1-58388-054-2

RECREATIONAL VEHICLES

RVs & Campers 1900-2000: An Illustrated History ISBN 1-58388-064-X
Ski-Doo Racing Sleds 1960-2003 Photo Archive ISBN 1-58388-105-0

AUTOMOTIVE

AMC Cars 1954-1987: An Illustrated History ISBN 1-58388-112-3
AMX Photo Archive: From Concept to Reality ISBN 1-58388-062-3
Auburn Automobiles 1900-1936 Photo Archive ISBN 1-58388-093-3
Camaro 1967-2000 Photo Archive ISBN 1-58388-032-1
Checker Cab Co. Photo History ISBN 1-58388-100-X
Chevrolet Corvair Photo History ISBN 1-58388-118-2
Chevrolet Station Wagons 1946-1966 Photo Archive ISBN 1-58388-069-0
Classic American Limousines 1955-2000 Photo Archive ISBN 1-58388-041-0
Cord Automobiles L-29 & 810/812 Photo Archive ISBN 1-58388-102-6
Corvair by Chevrolet Experimental & Production Cars 1957-1969, Ludvigsen Library Series ISBN 1-58388-058-5
Corvette The Exotic Experimental Cars, Ludvigsen Library Series ISBN 1-58388-017-8
Corvette Prototypes & Show Cars Photo Album ISBN 1-882256-77-8
Early Ford V-8s 1932-1942 Photo Album ISBN 1-882256-97-2
Ferrari- The Factory Maranello's Secrets 1950-1975, Ludvigsen Library Series ISBN 1-58388-085-2
Ford Postwar Flatheads 1946-1953 Photo Archive ISBN 1-58388-080-1
Ford Station Wagons 1929-1991 Photo History ISBN 1-58388-103-4
Hudson Automobiles 1934-1957 Photo Archive ISBN 1-58388-110-7
Imperial 1955-1963 Photo Archive ISBN 1-882256-22-0
Imperial 1964-1968 Photo Archive ISBN 1-882256-23-9
Javelin Photo Archive: From Concept to Reality ISBN 1-58388-071-2
Lincoln Motor Cars 1920-1942 Photo Archive ISBN 1-882256-57-3
Lincoln Motor Cars 1946-1960 Photo Archive ISBN 1-882256-58-1
Nash 1936-1957 Photo Archive ISBN 1-58388-086-0
Packard Motor Cars 1935-1942 Photo Archive ISBN 1-882256-44-1
Packard Motor Cars 1946-1958 Photo Archive ISBN 1-882256-45-X
Pontiac Dream Cars, Show Cars & Prototypes 1928-1998 Photo Album ISBN 1-882256-93-X
Pontiac Firebird Trans-Am 1969-1999 Photo Album ISBN 1-882256-95-6
Pontiac Firebird 1967-2000 Photo History ISBN 1-58388-028-3
Rambler 1950-1969 Photo Archive ISBN 1-58388-078-X
Stretch Limousines 1928-2001 Photo Archive ISBN 1-58388-070-4
Studebaker 1933-1942 Photo Archive ISBN 1-882256-24-7
Studebaker Hawk 1956-1964 Photo Archive ISBN 1-58388-094-1
Studebaker Lark 1959-1966 Photo Archive ISBN 1-58388-107-7
Ultimate Corvette Trivia Challenge ISBN 1-58388-035-6

AMERICAN CULTURE

Coca-Cola: A History in Photographs 1930-1969 ISBN 1-882256-46-8
Coca-Cola: Its Vehicles in Photographs 1930-1969 ISBN 1-882256-47-6
Phillips 66 1945-1954 Photo Archive ISBN 1-882256-42-5
American Service Stations 1936-1943 Photo Archive ISBN 1-882256-27-1

*THIS PRODUCT IS SOLD UNDER LICENSE FROM MACK TRUCKS, INC. MACK IS A REGISTERED TRADEMARK OF MACK TRUCKS, INC. ALL RIGHTS RESERVED.

All Iconografix books are available from direct mail specialty book dealers and bookstores worldwide, or can be ordered from the publisher. For book trade and distribution information or to add your name to our mailing list and receive a **FREE CATALOG** contact:
Iconografix, PO Box 446, Dept BK Hudson, WI, 54016 Telephone: (715) 381-9755, (800) 289-3504 (USA), Fax: (715) 381-9756

More great books from Iconografix

ISBN 1-58388-050-X

ISBN 1-58388-091-7

ISBN 1-58388-106-9

ISBN 1-58388-077-1

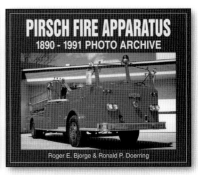

ISBN 1-58388-082-8

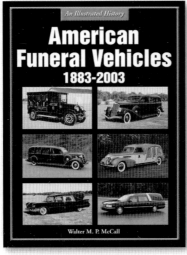

ISBN 1-58388-104-2

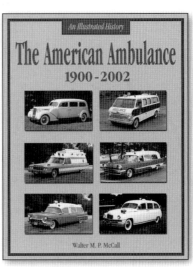

ISBN 1-58388-081-X

TABLE OF CONTENTS

DEDICATION

This book is dedicated to all the employees and workers that made Maxim what it was, one of the greatest fire truck builders in America, and to all the firefighters that were proud to say they drove and worked on a Maxim fire truck.

ACKNOWLEDGEMENTS

I'd like to thank many of the same people that helped with the first book – *Maxim Fire Apparatus Photo Archive 1914-1989*. It's impossible to list everyone, but please know that every phone call, letter and e-mail were helpful to the project. I'd like to especially thank Rich Louf – without him I would not have a Maxim photo collection. I'd also like to thank longtime Maxim employee and former owner David Deane for reviewing the material for accuracy as well as Richard Gergel for information on the Maxim-Ward LaFrance era. I'd also like to thank my family once again. There were many days when I would disappear into the basement and bang away on the keyboard for hours on end.

FOREWORD

When I started collecting information on Maxim back in the early 1990s, I wasn't sure what or how much information I would find. I was relatively new to the fire truck hobby and didn't even know where to start looking for information – but I stumbled along. It has been an exciting and interesting journey and I have met some fine people in the hobby with a sincere interest in preserving the history of fire apparatus, no matter what make or model, who would share information without hesitation. I hope this journey continues!

I was pleasantly surprised that the first Maxim book *Maxim Fire Apparatus Photo Archive 1914-1989* was so appreciated! I received a great deal of phone calls, letters and e-mails supporting the notion that a book on Maxim was long overdue. During my research the last few years, I was surprised to find out just how popular this small fire apparatus manufacturer from the northeast really was. Let it be known that Maxim has loyal fans all over the United States. Despite being a photo book,

it was still more than what was previously out in the literary field on Maxim, which was nothing. There was no single book dedicated to the Maxim Motor Company. With the exposure that I received from the photo book, I took all the information and feedback from everyone and tried to compile a more inclusive and comprehensive history on the company. I hope this book paints a more complete picture of what the company was all about and why they were so successful. I hope this one doesn't disappoint—I don't think it will.

After the release of the Maxim photo book, I had a great deal of requests from Maxim buffs to see some photos of newer style Maxim trucks. For many reasons there is a severe shortage of Maxim factory photos from the 1970s and up. Despite an intense search, I only managed to find about a dozen private shots of newer apparatus worthy of printing. Please note that I did the best I could with the photos I had to demonstrate the broad array of Maxim products produced over the years.

THE BEGINNINGS OF MAXIM

The surname Maxim is originally of English, French and German origin. Literally translated, it means "the greatest." The Maxim family settled in New England and has several branches in Massachusetts with others settling in Maine. The Maxim family has a long history of genius with many innovators and inventors in the bloodline. One close relative to Carlton W. Maxim, the founder of the Maxim Motor Company, was Hudson Maxim who invented a type of smokeless cannon powder and high explosives. Hudson's brother Hiram Stevens Maxim had his share of genius as he invented a type of fire extinguisher, water feed valves, methods to measure water pressure, and a type of automatic sprinkler system. However, he is better known for his invention of an automatic machine gun that was instrumental during World War I. The same basic design has not changed over the years and is used in modern weaponry today. Hiram's son, Hiram Percy Maxim, also picked up where the family left off with his own marvels that dealt mainly with sound suppression items such as car mufflers, air conditioners, and a gun silencer appropriately referred to as the Maxim Silencer. Even more interesting were his tinkerings with a successful "horseless carriage," or automobile, in 1898. Without a doubt, it's safe to say that the Maxim family was always ahead of their time.

Carlton W. Maxim was born in Carver, Massachusetts in 1859 to Nathan Bennett Maxim and Hulda (Atwood) Maxim. As a young man, Carlton worked with his father in a sawmill where he gained valuable knowledge in woodworking. While living in the East Middleboro section of town, he eventually established his own woodworking business on Vine Street. The woodworking business included the construction and repair of furniture, horse-drawn carriages, and interior finish work as well as the finish of slates. One of his main projects included the construction of wooden extension ladders – a knowledge that would prove very appropriate given his future endeavors.

The success of his business allowed Carlton to purchase one of the first motorized automobiles in the area, a 1901 Steamer. He quickly realized that his automobile needed maintenance and repairs. Born with the gift of being mechanically inclined, he quickly taught himself how to repair his car. Known for his attention to detail and incredible ingenuity it came as no surprise that soon other local car owners started bringing their cars to him to be repaired.

In 1906, the woodworking business was relocated and based out of the former New Bedford and Onset Railway barn at 24 Wareham Street. A few years later Carlton moved the woodworking business yet again to another building, the former Hathaway, Soule and Harrington factory on Cambridge Street where he continued with his successful business. The building at the former location of 24 Wareham Street was extensively remodeled and would eventually become the new home of what Carlton called the Middleborough

C. W. Maxim, Keith & Pratt Factory, Middleboro, Mass.

Before building fire trucks, Carlton Maxim was a successful carpenter with a successful woodworking business and factory.

Auto Exchange, a business he created to repair automobiles. The dates are questionable, but for some time he operated both the woodworking business and the automobile business simultaneously. Sometime around 1915, Carlton became one of the only automobile salesmen in southeastern Massachusetts selling cars out of the Middleborough Auto Exchange. At first, he sold only Auto-Cars, but would soon represent Corbin, E.M.F., Flanders, Studebaker, Willys-Knight, Overland, Mc-Farlan, and later on Dodge and Plymouth. Under the guise of the Middleborough Auto Exchange, Carlton also formed an automobile club similar to our modern day AAA. He also offered a unique service to the community and local residents – "a picnic conveyance or party barge." This automobile was a primitive bus that was used to take the local citizens to parties, tours or entertainment trips to Boston. In the new building he set up operations for carriage and automobile repair. The woodworking business continued to repair, repaint and manufacture wooden extension ladders.

Carlton was also very civic-minded and lent his services to other community needs. Carlton joined the Middleborough Fire Department as a firefighter around 1889. He started his career as a firefighter as a member of Hose Four on the West Side during the time of horse-drawn apparatus. It didn't take long for Carlton to make Captain and he was soon elected to the Board of Engineers. In 1912, he was elected Chief Engineer and then, in 1920, became Fire Chief of the reorganized department and remained Fire Chief until his resignation in 1929. While Fire Chief, Carlton was instrumental in the design and construction of a new head-quarters fire station on North Main Street in 1926, which still exists today.

Carlton eventually met and soon married Betsey Morse in the late 1800s and had two children whom would both play an active role in the family businesses. Ernest Leighton Maxim was born in July 1886. Carlton and Betsey also had a daughter named Elsie Maxim who would later marry Joseph Whitcomb. Joseph Whitcomb would hold several positions in the family company.

Ernest Maxim was raised in the local schools and upon completing his education went to work for his father as a bookkeeper in his father's mill. Throughout his career, like his father, Ernest would also be very active in civic affairs. He served as a member of the Board of Selectman and as a director at the Middleborough Trust Company. This would become an ironic note, as a loan from this very institution is what eventually brought about the end of the Maxim company. Ernest also served on the Board of Trustees at the nearby St. Lukes Hospital as well as on the local draft board.

Maxim started building fire apparatus on their own chassis a few short years after entering the fire apparatus business in the mid-teens. This unmarked combination chemical wagon and pumper was typical of apparatus built by Maxim in the late teens and into the early 1920s.

CHAPTER ONE

THE FIRST MAXIMS

In 1912, the Middleborough Fire Department purchased a Knox hose car. A few years later, in 1914, the department found the need for another fire truck. During the previous two years, many faults were discovered with the Knox. Maxim was unimpressed with the Knox and was very confident that he could not only build a second vehicle, but also improve on the features of the Knox truck. He submitted a proposal that he be given the opportunity to design and construct the next piece of motorized equipment for the department. The town leaders accepted his contract and right away he began work on this new piece of machinery. Thank goodness that conflict-of-interest and ethics laws were not what they are today, or the Maxim Motor Company would never have had its start.

Maxim used an E. R. Thomas Flyer chassis supplied by the E. R. Thomas Company, a well-established motorcar maker who supplied a special fire apparatus chassis to various other builders. This new truck was equipped with a 4-cylinder engine with a 4 1/2-inch bore and a 5-inch stroke. It also boasted pneumatic tires and chain drive. He added the other necessary features to make this truck exactly what the department was

looking for. These features included a hose bed capable of carrying 1,500 feet of 2 1/2-inch hose and two ground ladders – one 18-foot rope hoist extension ladder and one 12-foot roof ladder with folding hooks.

At a time when other fire departments were making the transition from horse-drawn steamers to motorized apparatus, Middleboro received its new truck. On May 12, 1914, the new truck, dubbed the Maxim Model "N," was delivered to the Middleborough Fire Department for the cost of $2,500. It took Maxim only 60 days to construct and deliver this unit as promised.

Stories of this new apparatus quickly spread throughout the area and New England, and soon several other local fire departments were requesting that Maxim build similar apparatus for them. Maxim began producing fire apparatus as the requests came in. He used more E. R. Thomas Flyer chassis for most of the early trucks. Some of these early trucks went to departments in Ansonia, Connecticut and Westerly, Rhode Island. Many of the first fire trucks were still being built under the name of the Middleborough Auto Exchange.

Like Middleboro, the Westerly Fire Department was looking for a fire truck that would serve a special purpose. They not only wanted a vehicle to carry hose but also wanted one powerful enough to pull their current steamer up some of the steepest hills in town. Upon its delivery, the truck was in fact driven up the steepest grade in town with Ernest Maxim at the wheel. There's a rumor that there was a verbal agreement that the 40-gallon chemical tank was to be filled with a popular Rhode Island beer upon delivery. This agreement was also honored.

In 1915, Maxim produced fire apparatus under the name of the Maxim Fire Apparatus Company. According to a letter from the Maxim Fire Apparatus Company to the purchasing agent for Skowhegan, Maine – Maxim offered two types of fire apparatus. Part of the letter described the options available on the two apparatus offered:

"Our F-4 single tank combination car has a 4-cylinder motor, 40-gallon chemical tank, body capacity for 1,200 feet of 2 1/2-inch hose, and all the usual fire equipment. This car is constructed of the best possible materials and labor and is in every way a high-grade piece of apparatus.

Our Type F-6 single tank combination car has a 6-cylinder motor, 40-gallon chemical tank, body capacity for 1,200 feet of 2 1/2–inch hose, and all the usual fire equipment. This car is of the same material and workmanship as our Type F-4 but has a more powerful motor and is proportionately heavier in construction.

Regarding prices of the above machines, we are able to build the Type F-4 with our standard equipment for about $4,200, and the Type F-6 for about $4,800."

With the increase in requests for apparatus came the need for additional staff and personnel. With the introduction of the Model F-6 and the hopes of introducing a ladder truck, they had to produce a heavy-duty truck. This heavy-duty truck needed a heavy-duty chassis and drive train. Maxim turned to one of their axle suppliers for help. The Sheldon Axle Plant sent one of their best engineers for several weeks to assist Maxim with layouts for their new product line. Charles A. (Bert) Carey arrived at Maxim in April 1915 at the age of 30. He was very experienced having worked for the well-known Matheson Motor Car Company as well as building racecars for Louis Chevrolet and having also worked for the Baldwin firm in the field of locomotives. Bert Carey never returned to the Sheldon Axle Plant and remained a faithful Maxim employee for over 50 years until his retirement in 1966. He held the position of Chief Engineer for most of his career. Many Maxim employees over the years remained faithful to the company, some staying with the firm for life. Another such employee, a Charles Kennedy, was a blacksmith by trade and also happened to be a neighbor to Carlton. In the early 1900s, Mr. Kennedy went to work for Maxim forging metal, first on the horse-drawn carriages and even later on the automobiles. Mr. Kennedy took a job in New York City with the promise given by Carlton that his job would be waiting should he return. After a period of time, and missing his family he left back in Middleboro, Mr. Kennedy returned from New York to his Maxim job where he remained for the rest of his life. The year 1915 also saw Maxim build their first motor pumping unit for the Hamden Fire Department in Hamden, Connecticut on an E. R. Thomas Flyer chassis with a 500-gallon-per-minute (gpm) pump. Other notable fire apparatus manufacturers of the time included Ahrens Fox, American LaFrance, Knox, Pirsch, Robinson, Seagrave and W. S. Nott.

In 1916, Maxim began the manufacture of his own fire truck chassis and discontinued using E. R. Flyers. Maxim also started

This single banked city service ladder truck with chemical tank was delivered to the Winthrop, Massachusetts fire department, northeast of Boston in 1917. Note the searchlight, wood spoke wheels and the lantern hanging near the cowl. *Photo courtesy of Dick Adelman Collection*

building trucks for the commercial trucking industry. These commercial trucks were a local commodity and were mostly sold and used in the southeastern Massachusetts area. Like the fire apparatus, these trucks were highly regarded for their dependability and quality. This venture only lasted a few years when Maxim decided to focus their efforts on the manufacture of fire apparatus. Maxim was a year or so ahead of his time using his own chassis, as the Ford Model T was probably the most commonly used fire apparatus across the nation at the time. This new Maxim apparatus had many features that made it desirable to many departments looking for fire apparatus. These new trucks included features such as 6-cylinder engines with Rumsey rotary gear pumps, worm drive axles instead of the chain-driven types and triple ignitions with three sets of spark plugs. Pneumatic tires, improved steering gears and improved suspensions for smoother rides impressed many customers and Maxims' reputation as dependable fire apparatus continued to grow throughout New England. One of the first city service ladder trucks was delivered to Winthrop, Massachusetts, a city northeast of Boston, in 1917.

With World War I underway in Europe, many of the established fire apparatus companies were awarded government contracts to supply fire apparatus for the protection of military installations both at home and abroad. Being a relatively new company, Maxim did not produce any apparatus for the military, but continued to maintain the quality of his products and strengthen the company. Up until this point, Carlton operated the business as an individual with the help of family and a small crew of employees. Mr. Maxim made a business decision to incorporate under the name of Maxim Motor Company. The

corporation issued common stock held by the Maxim family and a preferred stock, issued to provide additional capital, was absorbed by local businesses in town. The officers of the company consisted of: Carlton W. Maxim, President; Ernest L. Maxim, Treasurer (a skill he honed as a bookkeeper in his father's woodworking business years earlier); and Florence Swell, Clerk – all three comprising the Board of Directors. Joe Whitcomb (Carlton's son-in-law) would later join the board in 1935 and Leighton Maxim (Ernest's son) in 1951.

Maxim continued fine tuning his apparatus and produced three popular types of apparatus – the Model 6TN5, a triple combination pumper with 500-, 600- and 750-gpm capacities, a Model WHL6 city service ladder truck, and a Model T6 tractor.

The Model 6TN5 was a triple combination pump, chemical and hose truck. It had a pump rated at 500-gpm, a 6-cylinder engine, worm drive capable of 45 miles-per-hour (mph), a rotary gear pump, and a hose bed with a capacity of 1,000 to 1,200 feet of 2 1/2-inch hose.

The Model T6 tractor was also a 6-cylinder engine with worm drive, capable of speeds up to 35 mph with a 4-speed transmission. It was also noted that this tractor could be adapted to any horse-drawn apparatus. At least one tractor was sold to Waltham, Massachusetts and ran as a tillered ladder truck assigned as Ladder 2.

The Model WHL6 city service ladder truck, like the others, was also based on a 6-cylinder chassis with a 20-foot wheelbase. It was available with chemical tank or other equipment and a choice of pneumatic or solid tires. The buyer also had a choice of solid or trussed-type wooden ground ladders – a product that Maxim built himself using a skill honed over the last decade. The standard ladder truck was equipped with a 50-foot extension ladder, a 40-foot extension ladder, a 35-foot extension ladder, a 25-foot wall ladder, and roof ladders of 24, 22, 20, 16 and 13 feet in height. All three models had a guaranteed delivery date of 30 days and came in a dark red, almost maroon color (called Uzatona Red) with elaborate gold leaf, as most apparatus of the time did.

As requests came in for more apparatus, more room was needed to meet the growing demand. The car barn was remodeled and a second floor was added to provide an area where the paint shop could operate. The mill building on Cambridge Street was discontinued and the woodworking shop was also moved to the second floor. Having learned from one of the best (Carlton himself), woodworkers Dudley Perkins and Charles N. Warren established the Maxim ladder as one of the best in the industry. Carlton's exceptional woodworking craftsmanship was embedded into the construction of the wooden ladders needed for the fire apparatus and they easily married his affinity for woodworking with the automobile business. Maxim preferred the trussed type of ladder for its strength, but offered a solid beam ladder as well. The side rails of the ladders were constructed of air-seasoned, carefully selected Oregon Fir, and the rungs were made of second growth Hickory spaced 12 inches on center. Another Maxim feature was the fact that the rungs did not extend through the sides of the rail blocks, which provided a stronger bond and prevented decay.

Charles Warren also happened to be an avid photographer and snapped a photo of Ernest Maxim showing off his version of the Maxim ingenuity during the winter of 1918. Ernest built a homemade iceboat propelled by a 4-cylinder engine with a large single propeller in the rear. The photo was shown in a local newspaper showing the boat being used at nearby Assawompsett Pond on the Middleboro-Lakeville town line. According to the write-up by the reporter who witnessed the event, the iceboat was as sturdy as the fire apparatus Maxim produced. Unfortunately the poor quality of the photo prohibits the use of the photo in this book.

A large concrete assembly area was also added to the rear of the main building that extended out to Jackson Street. This is where the finishing touches were completed to each Maxim fire truck before sending it off to a fire department eagerly awaiting its new apparatus. Maxim's closest competitors at the time were probably the Buffalo Fire Appliance Corporation and the Sanford Motor Truck Company in nearby New York. A few years later, an upcoming local New England firm called D. E. McCann's and Sons Company of Portland, Maine would also compete for local business.

Maxim's unique gabled hood and chrome plated radiator gave them a look all their own. This nice looking 1924 Maxim Model C-2 350-gpm pumper that carries the serial number 556, belonged to Hingham, Massachusetts.

CHAPTER TWO

THE NEW MAXIMS

Maxim had finally gained a reputation for reliable and dependable fire apparatus, but that wasn't enough. They redesigned their apparatus with a distinctive new look that set them apart from the competition. In 1921, Maxim announced a new line of apparatus that included a "C" series and an "M" series chassis. Basically, the two models of apparatus were similar in design, but different in size. Both models featured McFarlan or Wisconsin engines and Northern rotary gear pumps. The smaller "C" model pumpers were powered by the 4-cylinder Wisconsin, and a 6-cylinder McFarlan engine drove the larger "M" models. Both had the distinctive Maxim gabled radiator and hood with vertical louvered vents located on the sides of the engine compartments. All vehicles were equipped with the trademark Maxim twin bucket seats and red and white enameled, or cloisonné style, Maxim logo on the top center of the radiator with a trademark Maxim "M." Windscreens were an option. The "C" model pumper was available with either a 350 (C-1 model), 400 (C-2 model) or 450-gpm (C-3) pump, and the Model "M" was equipped with either a 500 (M-1 model),

a 600 (M-2 model) or 750-gpm (M-3 model) pump. They also offered the CHL (4-cylinder) ladder truck or the MHL (6-cylinder) ladder truck with combined ladder footage of 255 feet. One easy way to tell the two models apart is to take a quick look at the radiator – the smaller "C" model chassis had a painted radiator shell while the larger "M" model chassis had the larger nickel-plated radiator shell. Other models available included the Model 6M Chemical and Hose combinations with a single chemical tank and three sizes of the Model M6 four-wheeled tractors in the product line. Chemical tanks were the full Holloway type with all-copper booster tanks. A year later, in 1922, Maxim offered a second size of the Chemical and Hose car with double chemical tanks, called the M-66.

Maxim was finally coming "into their own" and started distributing fire apparatus outside of New England. One of the first major sales agents outside of New England was the Woodhouse Manufacturing Company of New York. This distributor helped Maxim gain a foothold in the New York and New Jersey areas. A little further away from the northeast Maxim entertained several

Maxim archives showing a *Boston Herald* newspaper article dated November 4, 1951, concerning the 1920's Maxim pumpers still fighting fires in Tokyo, Japan.

Close-up and cross-section view of a Northern rotary pump commonly used in vintage Maxim pumpers in the 1920s. The numbers are there for obvious diagramming purposes, but there is no corresponding chart to go along with the photo.

inquiries on new apparatus from Tokyo, Japan. In a cable response, Maxim quoted, "quote on 750-gallon pumper, same as last model" to the never-ending inquiries. In 1925, one of every model made its way to the orient. The cost of a 1921 "M" model pumper varied depending on model and equipment, but the prices ranged from $8,000 to $11,000.

In an effort to broaden their sales area, Maxim advertised in many arenas to gain a firmer foothold in the industry. They embarked on a letter writing campaign sending letters to fire chiefs in the market for new apparatus and also advertised heavily in *The Fire Engineer* magazine. One great advertisement in 1925 featured a story about a 500-gallon pumper in Bridgewater, Massachusetts that pumped a 2 1/2-inch hose-line over 1,800 feet and single-handedly extinguished a house fire and saved the attached barn. If there's any doubt, actual photos of the scene were included showing the damaged home and the pumper off in the distance. Maxim also offered their own advertising in the form of testimonials from customers. One sales brochure supplied to fire departments in 1928 contained a letter and photos from the Fire Chief in Montpelier, Vermont who indicated that his two Maxim apparatus, a pumper and a ladder truck, were caught in a major flood in 1927 and submerged for over 36 hours. Upon request, Maxim immediately sent mechanics and tools, and by the next day the apparatus were back in service without any noticeable damage. Incidentally, the department used their third apparatus, a Maxim pumper, to pump out their municipal building — it pumped for 170 hours without stopping. The mechanics did a thorough check of that truck as well and no repairs or maintenance were necessary. As if the reputation that Maxim was building wasn't enough,

This is a 1928 city service ladder truck that saw service in Wrentham, Massachusetts. Maxim offered two sizes of city service ladder trucks in 1928. It is unclear which type this was. *Photo courtesy of Dick Adelman Collection*

they also provided their own newsletter titled *The Maxim FireGuard*, which was published from time to time "in the interest of better community fire protection." This newsletter offered glimpses into new products, recent apparatus deliveries and letter writing contests – presumably to be used for testimonials.

Production continued as usual during most of the 1920s with minor changes in company operations. However, to keep up with competition, the truck models available to the consumers were refined to meet customer's needs. So Maxim introduced a

new "B" model pumper in 1928. The "B" model pumpers were very similar to the "M" and "C" series pumpers in design and appearance, and Maxim replaced both to offer the customers several choices of one simplified design. Given the smaller size of the "C" models, Maxim chose to phase out the "C" models and replace them with the "B" model in several sizes. To avoid redundancy, the "M" model saw its exit as well. There was a 500-gpm model (the B-50), a 600-gpm (B-60), a 750-gpm model (the B-75) and a large 1,000-gpm model dubbed the B-10. With the new design

1929 Maxim pumper from Franklin, Massachusetts pictured in a more recent photo. The headlights and carbon dioxide extinguisher, along with other equipment, was not original. *Photo courtesy of Dick Adelman Collection*

came improvements in the accessories. The Northern rotary gear pump was replaced with a Hale or Maxim rotary gear pump with booster tanks. If requested, Maxim-built Holloway chemical tanks were still available. Each of the discharge lines was equipped with Maxim automatic relief valves. They also offered a Model GHL city service ladder truck or a smaller BHL town service ladder truck with ten other models of specialty vehicles available including forest fire trucks with 35-, 50- and 100-gallon capacities. Buda engines supplied the power in the 1920s vintage "B" series trucks and on into the early 1930s series trucks. Maxim was now becoming a major contender in the field of fire apparatus

manufacturing with many sales agents all over the East Coast. The metro-Boston area was covered by the Arthur H. Blanchard Company out of Cambridge, Massachusetts and with coverage in southern New England by Joseph L. Kelly of Pawtucket, Rhode Island. Maxim's hometown of Middleboro purchased one of the new "B" model pumpers in 1928 – a B-75 750-gpm pumper. This unit demonstrated many of the modern features that surpassed the other makes currently on the market – "a 6-cylinder, 125 horsepower Buda engine capable of speeds up to 50 mph and four-wheel mechanical brakes with vacuum booster. It also featured a Hale rotary pump, an auxiliary pump

Nahant, Massachusetts was the proud owner of this 1932 Maxim city service ladder. This angle shows the flat-faced radiator commonly found on this model. Note the black and gold Maxim emblem and elaborate gold leafing on the fenders.

cooling system for extended pumping jobs and a powerful lighting system for night-time work."

The Manchester By-the-Sea Fire Department in Massachusetts purchased one of these pumpers in 1929. According to department records, the department was looking into replacing an aging hose wagon or supplementing it with an additional, more modern, piece of apparatus. The department journal on April 9, 1929, read as follows: "The town does need this second piece of apparatus and the Fire Engineers believe that a new hose piece should be purchased. This may be either a new hose wagon or a combined hose wagon and pumper of somewhat smaller capacity than the Seagrave. A good hose wagon alone can be purchased for $6,000. This same piece fitted with a pump, which can handle 600 gpm will cost $8,000. The Fire Engineers believe that proper fire protection of the Town would best be served by the combined pump and hose wagon...."

A side view of this 1932 ladder truck from Uxbridge, Massachusetts shows the overhang of the ground ladders off the rear of the truck. Uxbridge purchased a twin Maxim pumper the same year.

Another journal entry a few days later on Sunday, April 14, 1929, followed "...the Board of Fire Engineers made a trip to Maxim Fire Apparatus factory at Middleboro and inspected factory and apparatus..." The next day, the engineers decided to purchase a Maxim pumper, "...having come to the conclusion that it was the best they could get for the price...." At the time of this writing, this unit is still around and privately owned. It was eventually traded by Manchester for a newer apparatus in 1963 and was purchased in used condition by the North Coventry, Rhode Island

department. Sometime thereafter, it was purchased yet a second time and restored by the Crystal Lake Fire Department in Ellington, Connecticut. The truck has been caringly restored and spends its time winning trophies at shows and parades.

With more and more motorized vehicles becoming popular in the United States, the storage and use of gasoline was more widespread. Since water alone could not be used to fight petroleum-based fires, Maxim offered a Fomon foam system on their equipment. Maxim had an arrangement with the American Fomon Company of Drexel, Pennsylvania to supply foam fire extinguishers, or the Model 12 Fomon foam generator. Typically this unit was mounted on the apparatus, but if needed away from the apparatus it could be connected within a hose line via two-in-one couplings that allowed a variety of hose sizes without disconnecting the unit. The one container of foam solution, the equivalent of a 40-gallon tank, was poured into the hopper and mixed into the hose-line where it was deployed when needed. This portable set-up kept the booster tanks free of foam.

The Stock Market crash in 1929 sent America into a frenzy and most businesses into panic. The economy was weakening and it would only get worse. Maxim, like other businesses, was affected during the lean years, but never had to walk the financial tightrope. At the time, Ernest Maxim and Bert Carey were in Europe studying European ladder designs as they had high hopes of introducing an aerial ladder to the product line. The weakening economy put this project on hold until a more opportune time. Carlton retired as Fire Chief in

Milton, Massachusetts still owns this 1933 750-gpm pumper. This Model 32C pumper had a 100-gallon tank and was serial number 776.

The hometown of Maxim, Middleboro was a large user of Maxim apparatus for obvious reasons. This 1934 500-gpm pumper is proudly owned by the Middleboro Historical Society.

1929, possibly to devote his full attention to guiding his company through the rough financial waters.

Always a family institution, the company saw several more family members join the firm in 1930. Leighton L. Maxim (Ernest's son) and Joseph C. Whitcomb (Carlton's son-in-law) came onboard and served in several positions over the years. Despite the stock market crash plunging the United States into the Great

Depression, it actually affected businesses differently throughout the fire apparatus industry. With other smaller competitors going out of business, Maxim held on. In fact, in 1932 they felt a need to improve the lines of apparatus currently offered. Taking into consideration that most fire departments could not and would not buy apparatus as luxuriously as they had in the past few years, Ernest Maxim took the initiative to develop a new line of re-designed apparatus hoping to stay competitive in the market. These new models had a conservative look while the fire apparatus industry as a whole started leaning towards the streamlined look. The new models boasted rounded hoods and flat-faced radiator shells, full crowned fenders and four hinged doors along the side of the engine compartment, replacing the former louvered type. These doors, often chromed, would become a common identifying mark for years to come. They sported the standard Maxim twin bucket seats and, like other fire apparatus of the day, windshields were becoming standard equipment. Another design change was the Maxim logo from the white and red enamel style to a black background with gold writing that spelled out "MAXIM." A Hercules 6-cylinder engine powered this new series, with Hale pumps available in capacities from 500 gpm up to 1,000 gpm. There were many different sizes to choose from including a W-50 and Y-50 with 500-gpm pumps, the R-60, R-75, H-74, H-75 with 750-gpm pumps, and the H-10 and H-10S with 1,000-gpm pumps. They also offered the 12 distinct models of "Y", "H" and "R" model single and double-banked city service ladder trucks. Costs for these pumpers ranged between $5,000 for the smaller pumpers and $11,000 for the larger pump sizes. This bold new design would not only keep Maxim in close proximity to its competition, but would also force the other competitors to keep pace with Maxim. Maxim, like other fire apparatus manufacturers, also offered fire apparatus on commercial chassis such as Ford, Chevrolet, Diamond T, REO and Studebaker.

The early 1930s saw even more changes with the Maxim firm. Maxim continued their plans of designing and building a hydraulic aerial ladder in 1933 despite the fact that Maxim competitor Peter Pirsch

A shop photo of a Hercules engine and Spicer transmission found in the Y-50 model pumpers of the 1930s.

made history by introducing the first patented mechanical aerial ladder hoist using hydraulic cylinders. In a letter dated November 1933 Ernest Maxim replies to a local Fire Chief's inquiry on whether Maxim had any plans of introducing an aerial ladder to the market:

"The reason I prefer to leave our company out of the situation is that we prefer not to place before our competitors, through the chiefs, a too complete knowledge of our plans, as any sales we make would be through our friends, at least in the beginning. You might, however, comment on the fact that it has come to your attention that a manufacturer is preparing to place on the market a new type of aerial truck which will embody many features of advantage, such as less overall length, less cost, and designed to meet the small city and big town requirement which as yet has not been well provided for in the present design of aerial ladders."

In 1935 Carlton retired from the Maxim Motor Company. His son Ernest succeeded him as President, Joseph Whitcomb took the reigns as Treasurer, and N. A. Shaw

Even though Maxim started producing their own chassis years earlier, that didn't prevent them from using commercial chassis. This early 1930s Ford AA chassis was used to build a hose wagon for a United States Navy base in Hingham, Massachusetts. Similar units built on Ford AA chassis were delivered to Wareham, Massachusetts and Dublin, New Hampshire.

took over as the Service Manager. Shortly after leaving the company, as if it were his lifeblood, Carlton Maxim passed away on August 27, 1935. He died in his home on Forest Street at the age of 76. According to his obituary he was described as "a successful and clear-sighted businessman, a pioneer in the automobile industry, an efficient and courteous town official and an outstanding citizen." Just in case there was any doubt as to the character of the man, it was also mentioned, "As in any of

his business dealings, he never made an important decision without careful study and when his decision was made he stood back of it to the end. His courage and honesty were never questioned in his decisions and if anybody hoped to hoodwink him in any of his deliberations which he thought were right they were hopelessly disappointed, for he carried with him always his early training in honest business relations." In regards to his products, "...the efficiency of the Maxim truck became recognized and

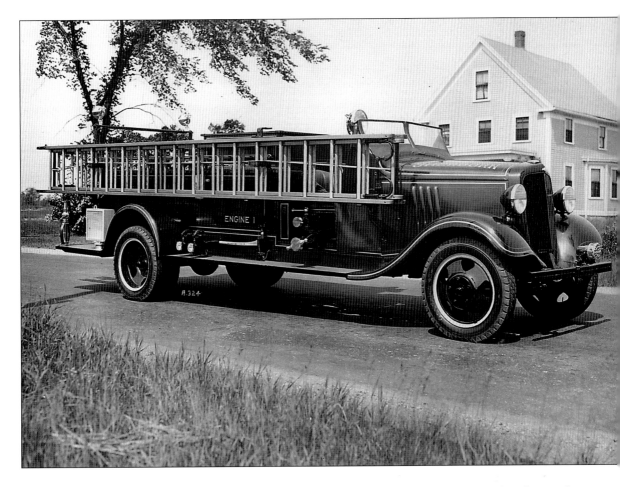

Sherborn, Massachusetts owned this 1934 pumper on a Chevrolet chassis. This truck is now privately owned in Massachusetts.

today equipment of this make are part of the fire departments of New England, the mid-Atlantic states, as well as far off as Japan." Former Middleboro Fire Chief George A. Philbrook speaking in 1936 of Carlton Maxim said, "He established a reputation for honest and efficient business methods, and was held in the very high esteem among his social and civic contacts. His devotion to the fire department set a standard of loyalty to duty, which was an outstanding example of his entire life. To know him was to love him. To serve under him was a privilege of great value, and as a valued friend and associate he is missed by all that knew him." This former fire chief and pioneer builder of fire apparatus had certainly left his mark on the industry and left a legacy for his family to continue.

The Maxim Motor Company carried on without Carlton by fine-tuning some of the details on the current line of fire truck apparatus. The chassis design remained fairly consistent but with some minor changes to

HEAVY DUTY
TRUCKS

MAXIM MOTOR COMPANY - Middleboro, Mass.

One little known fact about Maxim was their venture into the commercial trucking industry. Maxim built a freight truck on a 1938 Ford chassis. This Model F35 had a 3-½ ton rating and was available with a choice of three different lengths of body; 12-foot, 14-foot or 16-foot. It was also available in either a box or rack body. Allegedly, many of these units were used all over southeastern Massachusetts.

the radiator and hood designs this fire apparatus, along with other manufacturers, began to get larger and resemble the fire trucks that we know today. This slightly restyled apparatus featured a mild V-shaped grille with vertical center bar and a matching V-type windshield similar to Seagraves of the same era. At the reasonable price for a standard pumper costing between $6,500 and $8,500, many of these trucks were now becoming economical. Many of the trucks in the late 1930s and early 1940s appear

to be hybrids as Maxim experimented with different components such as radiators, hoods, cabs and doors. A combination of different parts gave vehicles of the same vintage slightly different looks. One of the advantages to custom-built fire apparatus was the ability to build the specific unit to meet the customer's needs. Custom-built fire apparatus were some of the finest made trucks available, and they were priced accordingly. Some of the other more popular custom fire apparatus builders of the time included Ahrens Fox, American LaFrance, Pirsch, Mack, Seagrave and Stutz. On the late 1930s and early 1940s apparatus, the Maxim logo made a change back from its black and gold insignia to its original form with the red and white cloisonné type. Depending on the make of the truck, it could be found in the upper right corner of the grille, or along the sides of the hoods on commercial vehicles.

As motorized vehicles became more and more popular, high-speed accidents became more frequent. Most fire apparatus manufacturers saw the need to keep the firefighters safe while responding to fires. Throughout the industry, the need for doors, semi-enclosed cabs and enclosed cabs were becoming more common on fire apparatus—and Maxim was no exception. Closed cabs were even more popular with firefighting personnel throughout New England and the northern states when fighting fires during cold winter months. One such truck was a 1936 500-gpm pumper delivered to the U.S. War Department in Eastport, Maine to protect the government housing at the Passamaquoddy Project. An article in the *Middleboro Gazette* in 1936 stated:

"The cab is something very new for fire apparatus, although it has been an indispensable unit in motor truck design for many years, fire apparatus has not used

Very little is known about this early 1940s dump truck on an REO chassis. Being a Maxim photo, it is likely that this was also part of their commercial truck line, or built for use around the Maxim facility.

this protective design heretofore. All of the instruments for operating the pumper are enclosed in the cab and entirely protected from the weather. This includes such items as the gauges, which at extreme low temperatures are apt to freeze and become useless. In the northern country where sub-zero temperature is an everyday condition during the winter months, the cab is the special feature as it provides protection not only for some of the delicate instruments but also the operator in charge of the truck and his assistant."

Some of the other features on this particular apparatus included "ground grip tires" and an overhead superstructure capable of carrying up to four ground ladders that allowed for more equipment storage on the apparatus body itself. The pump gauges were mounted inside the cab on the dashboard. On other models, pump gauges could also be found on the exterior of the truck located on the rear of the cab.

The 1930s were overall fairly bleak years for the fire apparatus manufacturing industry. Sales remained average throughout the

The first metal aerial produced by Maxim was this 1939 65-foot aerial delivered to the Advance Base Depot in Davisville, Rhode Island. Unconfirmed rumors have it that this truck was originally slated for Boston, Massachusetts but with the war looming the government "procured" it for military use. A similar rig was also delivered to Naval Air Station Miramar in San Diego, California.

late 1930s and the company looked for other ventures to try and boost profits. Taking a page from the history books back in 1916, Maxim tried their hand at commercial trucks again in 1938. Maxim constructed a freight truck on a Ford 2-ton chassis. Called the Model F-35, this truck boasted a 22,000-pound gross vehicle weight and was constructed using a highly reworked Ford cab and chassis with a beefed-up frame, 95 horsepower engine and Ford ignition system. Additional features included

Budd 10 stud wheels, oversized 8.5 x 20 tires, Ross steering gear, Lockheed brakes, Timken axles and special heavy-duty springs. The available body lengths were to include 12-, 14- and 16-foot lengths with either freight or stake bodies available. The F-35A had the smallest wheelbase at 158 inches, the F-35B at 176 inches and the F-35C the longest at 194 inches. It is unknown how many of these trucks were produced. At least one demonstrator was built, and it is believed that these trucks

A rear view of Advance Base Depot's aerial shows a compliment of trussed type aluminum ground ladders.

were popular and distributed throughout the New England area. It is also interesting to note that the Maxim Motor Company was not the only "Maxim" in the commercial trucking industry. A distant relative of Carlton Maxim, Hiram Percy Maxim, mentioned earlier, founded a company called Maxim Tricar Manufacturing in Thomasville, Connecticut as well as Maxim Tri-Car Company of Port Jefferson, New York in the early 1900s. These firms were involved with 1-, 2-, and 3 1/2-ton truck chassis as well

as farm tractors. Somewhere along the lines, a third company, Maxim Munitions Corporation of New York, was also owned and operated by Hiram Maxim in New York. Their most popular vehicle was the Maxim-Dart farm tractor.

Maxim continued their quest to develop an aerial ladder truck. Despite the setback during the early 1930s Maxim never lost interest and in 1939 finally built their first metal aerial ladder. There are unconfirmed reports that this first unit was originally

A nice view of an early 1940s chrome radiator on an unidentified ladder truck. Note the change back to the standard red and white Maxim emblem in the upper corner from the earlier black and gold emblem of the 1930s.

ordered by the City of Boston. However, with certain activities going on around the world, the citizens and government of the United States could sense that U.S. involvement in World War II was imminent. The government was boosting its resources and this truck was given government priority and subsequently was redirected to the Advance Base Depot, a U.S. Navy installation in Davisville, Rhode Island. This move towards producing an aerial ladder truck would turn out to be the first step in the right direction, as the Maxim Motor Company would later become very well known throughout the world for their metal aerial ladders.

Another interesting story regarding government equipment and the impending war occurred in the late 1930s. A rugged forest fire vehicle, a four-wheel drive brushbreaker, was ordered by the Town of Wareham to be used for fighting forest fires in the sandy Cape Cod terrain. The Ford chassis was

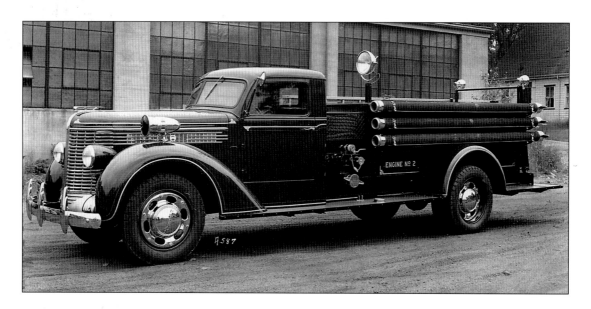

Who can resist admiring the fine lines on this 1940s vintage Diamond T? This factory photo, taken just behind the factory building, shows a well-built truck for the Wells Corner Hose Company. Diamond T was a popular truck chassis for all truck manufacturers in the 1940s.

Departments like Falmouth, Massachusetts would soon have the option of a metal aerial instead of this 1938 city service ladder truck. This Model 32L had a great white-over-red paint job and was serial number 838.

delivered to Maxim and work was soon to begin on its construction. The government began preparing and storing supplies in case they joined the war effort and four-wheel drive vehicles were a high priority in that stockpiling. Fearing that the government would seize their brand new, yet unfinished truck as "essential to the war effort," some local Wareham firefighters made their way to the Maxim plant and drove their unfinished truck back to Wareham where it was stored in a private barn for safekeeping. When the scare was over, or at least the federal authorities declared there would be no taking of four-wheel drive trucks, the truck was returned to Maxim so the work could be completed. It is certain that someone of authority at the Maxim firm had to have known about the location of the truck. This story was related to me by a reputable source, and when the story is told it's known locally as "the Midnight Requisition."

All branches of the armed forces received equipment from Maxim as well as many other fire apparatus manufacturers. The U.S. Navy received this FFN-5 crash truck on a 1944 International chassis. Note the six ground-sweep nozzles under the front bumper as well as the large hand-operated turret on the roof. This unit carried 800 gallons of water and 80 gallons of foam. Surprisingly, this unit did not have a pump-and-roll capacity.

CHAPTER THREE

THE WAR YEARS

America entered World War II on December 7, 1941. As we all know, that date was the bombing of Pearl Harbor and subsequently the beginning of United States involvement in World War II. For the few years before, most Americans knew that United States involvement was imminent. The war itself had no major negative impact on the Maxim company or its products. The only drawback was the rationing of the raw materials needed for construction. In fact, the war gave a boost to the economy and increased jobs desperately needed to aid the war effort. The fire apparatus industry was no exception. The government demanded additional supplies. Maxim, along with many other fire apparatus manufacturers, answered the call and produced a large quantity of mechanized goods including military fire trucks that protected shipyards and military and defense installations. Maxim also built marine pumping units, hundreds of trailer-mounted pumpers, nearly 2,000 saltwater distillation units, and many other sub-contract orders. This increase in work required new buildings, plant facilities and additional employment.

Many fire apparatus companies produced light trailer-type fire pumps, which could be pulled by a standard passenger car. Many of these trailers were manufactured by such prominent companies as the Labour Company of Elkhart, Indiana; the Sealand Corporation of Saugatuck, Connecticut and the Ralph B. Carter Company of Hackensack, New Jersey. Maxim, however, was one of the largest manufacturers of pumps during the war years, distributing hundreds of these trailer pumps officially called the "Emergency Defense Trailer" by Maxim. They were more commonly referred to by nicknames such as the "Blitz Buggy," the "Liberty Trailer" and the "Victory Trailer." These trailer-type stirrup pumps were manually operated and were intended for use by Civil Defense corps to fight incendiary bomb and other related fires. These trailers were to be stationed in strategic areas to be used in the event standard fire apparatus could not maneuver through destroyed areas throughout the community. According to Maxim literature in 1941, the trailers built by Maxim were offered in three sizes:

•500-gpm Underwriters' rating with Ford engine, 85 horsepower; pump, single stage, direct connected.

Detailed photos of a skid mounted pumping unit. Maxim offered two sizes of portable pumps. A 150-gpm pump powered by a 4-cylinder 25 horsepower engine with either centrifugal or rotary pump and a 25-gpm pump powered by a single engine 3 ½ horsepower engine with rotary pump.

•600-gpm Underwriters' rating with Ford Mercury engine, 95 horsepower; pump, single stage centrifugal, direct connected.

•750-gpm Underwriters' rating with Ford Zephyr engine, 120 horsepower; pump, single stage centrifugal, direct connected.

The private industry also took advantage of these new designs. Nashua Manufacturing Company, a textile mill in Nashua, New Hampshire, purchased one of these trailers to protect their facility.

Maxim also supplied several hundred military fire engines including foam pumpers and the standard structural pumpers that went to military installations all over the United States. Maxim, like other manufacturers, almost exclusively built fire apparatus for the war effort, with only a handful of extremely needy municipal departments receiving fire apparatus if they could prove a substantial hardship. Just one of many large military orders

that Maxim filled was a one-time contract for the United States Army for 47 pumpers built on Chevrolet chassis with USA truck identification numbers from 501718 through 501765.

The United States Army alone had specifications for three trailer-type apparatus and 12 distinct models of fire trucks used at Army installations in the United States. Maxim produced four of these 12 models. They included a Class 325 two-wheel drive 300-gpm pumper, a Class 325 four-wheel drive 300-gpm pumper, a Class 500 two-wheel drive 500-gpm pumper, and a Class 750 two-wheel drive 750-gpm pumper. Five of these Maxim 750-gpm pumpers were loaded onto a rail car in Middleboro and shipped to the U.S. Army Corp of Engineers in Missouri on April 1, 1941.

However, the Army wasn't the only branch of the armed services to use Maxim apparatus. Maxim built many foam trucks to U.S. Navy specifications. One particular model, the FFN-5 was built on

A great example of World War II-era firefighting equipment was this Emergency Defense Pumper, also labeled by Maxim as "Blitz Buggies." Maxim offered these trailer-type pumps, designed after units used in England, in three sizes: a 500 gpm pump powered by an 8 cylinder Ford engine, a 600 gpm pump powered by a Ford Mercury V-8 engine and a 750 gpm pump powered by a twelve cylinder Ford Zephyr engine. Many of these units were built and used by both public and private fire departments.

an International chassis and carried 800 gallons of water and 80 gallons of foam. The FFN-5 was an unusual rig for its time as it was capable of mixing the foam in the main tank. The water tank was partially filled and the foam entered through the bottom of the tank. A "churn valve" was then used to mix the contents. The unit had a Hale-Chrysler 500-gpm pump, but interestingly enough without pump-and-roll capabilities. The turret was manually operated from a platform on the roof of the truck. It also had six under-bumper ground sweep nozzles, each one having 20-gpm discharge

capabilities. Besides Maxim, the Fire Appliance Company and John Bean also built some of these identical units.

The other popular wartime truck was the Maxim Model X-50 with a 500-gpm pump. It was a standard pumper on any available commercial or custom chassis. One of these trucks was a 1942 Chevrolet pumper that was stationed at an ordinance plant in Eagan, Minnesota. After the war, the plant was dismantled and the truck transferred to a University of Minnesota Research Station that took over the property. In 1963, the Eagan Volunteer Fire Department was

A rather remarkable photo shows at least 10 military units staged in front of the main Maxim building. There are only a handful of factory photos in existence that were taken in front of the main building on Wareham Street. Two interesting details in this photo include the gas pumps visible in the center of the photo and the pair of feet visible underneath the truck in the foreground.

formed and they purchased this vehicle for $2,157. It is still owned by the department and affectionately referred to as, "Jenny." Also, in 1942, the Town of Southborough, Massachusetts purchased a 1942 Maxim with a 750-gpm pump. When they replaced it with a newer Maxim in 1971, this truck went up on the auction block. Locally famous Boston Pops conductor and fire buff, Arthur Feidler, later auctioned it off. During the war most private or municipal fire apparatus orders were deferred and

priority was given to government orders. It was rare for a town to get new apparatus during the early 1940s.

One unique wartime apparatus produced by Maxim that probably never made it past the prototype stage was that of a pump unit mounted on a motorcycle chassis. Using a three-wheeled Indian motorcycle with chain-on-shaft drive, Maxim engineers mounted a 500-gpm skid-mount pump coupled to an 85-horsepower Ford V-8 engine. After the initial construction,

This photo shows the same lot of trucks, but numbering 16 in this photo, lined up along Wareham Street—ready to be shipped wherever they were needed to support our country at war! Both Chevrolet and Ford chassis are visible in the lineup.

the chassis and pump were enclosed with a body borrowed from the "Emergency Defense Trailer" to make it complete. We may never know if this design was ever produced and if not, why, but we do know that other manufacturers, like Foamite-Childs built similar units like the "Indian Fire Patrol" with great success. These units were used successfully during the bombing raids in England to maneuver around collapsed buildings and fallen debris. It was also thought that in the event of a widespread attack on the United States, volunteers could use these small units—like the trailer type—in more areas.

To keep up with the high demand, additional property was acquired in 1942, just down the street from the main facility. This building belonged to the former Nemasket Automobile Company and was located adjacent to the Lincoln property on Wareham Street. This property was purchased from John Howes when he retired from his repair business. The buildings were modified slightly and the new property served as the repair and service department for the automobile business. This freed up some much needed room at the main plant and left the entire building to be used exclusively for the construction of fire apparatus. Maxim took on the additional task of repairing and servicing other makes and models of fire apparatus in addition to Maxims. Charles L. Norton organized the service department and when he retired, Merrill A. Shaw replaced him.

This front mount pumper on a Ford chassis was based on an Army standard that required a 4 x 2 chassis and 500-gpm pumper truck. According to a U.S. Army war manual its purpose was, "*Used by Corps of Engineers for combating structural fires at posts, camps and stations.*"

Same truck, different view. Notice the lack of equipment.

Close-up of the front mount pump.

Maxim experimented with this World War II vintage motorcycle type firefighting apparatus. They started with an Indian motorcycle chassis, a Ford V-8 engine and a 500-gpm skid-mount pump to get a small compact pumper on a maneuverable chassis. It's not known if any were actually produced or if this was just a prototype. This photo was taken indoors at the factory.

The finished product! Dubbed the "Emergency Defense Pumper," the body was borrowed from a portable pump trailer that was also mass-produced during the war effort. It is believed that these motorcycles were to be used like the ones in Britain during the German bombing raids, to maneuver around fallen buildings and debris, and they were produced with that in mind.

Most fire trucks made during the war years were for military and wartime use. A municipal department had to prove a hardship in order to receive new fire apparatus. Milton, Massachusetts south of Boston was fortunate enough to receive this streamlined 1942 sedan style 750-gpm pumper. If you look closely, you'll notice the Maxim insignia painted on the front wheel hub.

Westbrook, Connecticut also received a pumper during the mid-1940s. All of the brightwork, excluding the bumper, is painted instead of being chromed.

Delivered to the Wareham Fire District in Massachusetts in December 1946, this closed cab Model 2405 carries serial number 1516. This was one of the new style chassis to hit the market after the war. This pumper has a 500-gpm Hale pump and a 200-gallon booster tank. It's currently owned by the author and is undergoing a slow restoration. The truck now carries much of the original equipment.

CHAPTER FOUR

POSTWAR YEARS

The war ended a few years later and in 1945 several million dollars worth of contracts were cancelled leaving an order for 80 newly designed airfield crash vehicles. These crash vehicles could be found protecting most of the major airports on the East Coast as well as down south and out west. These medium-sized crash units, dubbed Airport-Turnpike Rescue Trucks, went to aircraft manufacturing facilities like Lockheed, Grumman, Fairchild and the Glen Martin Company in Maryland. Maxim concentrated their efforts in hopes of picking up the civilian production line where it left off just before the war.

Despite being busy with wartime production, the company had the foresight to design and develop a new line of re-styled trucks during 1944 and 1945, to be released when the peacetime operations resumed. This new line was started promptly after the war was over and the first of the new trucks were produced and delivered in January 1946. This new line of apparatus would become the mainstay for Maxim over the next 13 years. The chassis featured a wider cab with low, full

width V-type windshield and the fenders were redesigned with rounded corners. The fenders were purchased from the Chicago Manufacturing Company, in business since 1910. Interestingly, in the late 1940s Chicago Manufacturing sold a lot of the same fenders to the Sanford Motor Truck Company. A quick glance at a Sanford fire truck at the time might have stopped fire truck aficionados in their tracks, as these trucks looked quite a bit like Maxim trucks. Maxim also purchased truck cabs from the same firm. The rounded, half-moon type grille design with vertical style is what set Maxim apart from the other types of apparatus of the day. Pump sizes were available in 500-, 750-, 1,000- and even 1,250-gpm capacities. Cabs were available with several options for seating a minimum of three firefighters, a canopy style that seated up to seven firefighters or even a four-door model that also seated seven firefighters. The flexibility to mix and match features on most pumpers gave many communities the ability to design a truck to meet their specific needs. For instance, they could choose the cab style/seating arrangement; pump

After the war, Maxim introduced a newly designed apparatus in 1946 in hopes of resuming private orders and business. This sales drawing is an example of what was used in sales literature during the late 1940s to introduce a new product.

size, open or enclosed pump panel, compartmentation, etc. These trucks utilized Hercules gas engines, Spicer transmissions and Hale pumps. In the past, Maxim had model designations for each of their apparatus such as the "C" model pumper or the MHL city service ladder truck. This conventional chassis had model numbers to delineate between pumpers, sizes and types, but it is often erroneously referred to as a "J" model chassis. It is believed that Seagrave offered a "J" model chassis, and that Maxim did not.

In the world of fire apparatus, the postwar models were more improved modern pieces of equipment with such mechanical amenities as power steering and automatic transmissions. In some cases, some fire departments started installing two-way radios in their apparatus to make communication much easier as well as installing breathing apparatus that was primarily created and used during the war.

Maxim products were gaining a reputation for their leadership in craftsmanship and design, and the business continued to prosper. Also during 1946, with Maxim's reputation growing tremendously in the east, they started to branch strongly on the West Coast by joining up with L. N. Curtis and Sons of Oakland, California. L. N. Curtis would become a main distributor

If only some of these trucks could talk, the stories they could tell! This photo shows the author's 1946 Maxim pumper in the right bottom corner fighting a major fire in the midst of Hurricane Carol on August 31, 1954, in Wareham, Massachusetts. The hurricane caused flooding of up to four feet. The firefighters were later commended, *"The fireman used saltwater pumped from the street and all who witnessed the gallant manner of these men in the performance of their duty, have something to remember. Shoulder high in water; pulling hose, climbing ladders and holding hose nozzles until the heat became so intense that a few jumped from the roof into the water on the street. A performance that rated the cover of a book." Photo courtesy of Wareham Fire Department Archives*

for the West Coast with branch offices in Oakland, California, Salt Lake City, Utah and Seattle, Washington. Maxim would send the chassis to Curtis and then the Seattle branch would contract with the George Heiser Company of Seattle to do the bodywork. There were many Maxim/Curtis/Heiser rigs throughout the northwest. As in the east, Maxim ladders were highly regarded and in the 1960s you could find Maxim aerials mounted on Crown and Kenworth chassis in addition to the occasional Maxim

A typical Hercules engine that powered the new style of fire apparatus coupled with a 4-speed Spicer transmission. Maxim used a variety of Hercules engines depending on the sizes of the vehicles, and the power needed including WX, RX and HX series engines.

chassis. In later years, L. N. Curtis would also become a dealer for Ward LaFrance, a soon to be Maxim "cousin."

Maxim eventually garnered an even larger percentage of the fire truck market and soon was one of the top major producers of fire apparatus in America. Despite building their first aerial ladder in the late 1930s, they did not actually market the line of steel aerial ladders until 1947. Their all-steel Maxim aerial ladders were revolutionary and again forced other competitors to change and improve upon their own products to keep pace. The ladders were so well renowned that the aerial production line was expanded to allow the use of Maxim aerial ladders to be used by other manufacturers who did not build their own ladders, mainly Ward LaFrance and Mack.

Maxim fire trucks were soon finding customers on the West Coast. This late 1940s pumper was one of several that belonged to the Ripon Rural Fire Department in California.

The many body and cab styles gave prospective customers many options to choose from. Richmond, Indiana chose for their department this four-door pumper with seven-man cab and enclosed pump panel.

This 1950 Model 1417 semi-cab pumper belonged to Wareham, Massachusetts. Its 750-gpm pump was plenty to supply the deck gun mounted behind the cab. It was serial number 1739 and is privately owned but its condition is unknown.

Elkins Park, Pennsylvania owned another fine looking 1950 open cab pumper. Two unusual features about this truck are the light-colored paint scheme contrasted with the red rims, and the couplings near the pump panel. If you look closely, the couplings on the intakes as well as the adapters mounted on the running board appear to have some sort of quick-connect, or cam-lock type couplings.

Maxim's conventional chassis was popular from 1946 until 1960 with the introduction of the "F" and the "S" series. This 1953 pumper from Woodbridge, New Jersey served the Hopelawn Fire Department and was equipped with portable generator and large flood/search lights. It was serial number 1909.

A department with more than adequate staffing needed seating for all its manpower. Lexington, Kentucky chose this canopy cab style pumper with seating for seven with a bench seat to the rear of the cab.

In the 1960s Crown would join the list of fire truck builders using Maxim aerials.

In this new line was the newly designed Maxim middle-mount aerial ladder. The metal ladders were available in 65-foot, 75-foot, and 85-foot lengths in three sections. They were initially offered on straight frames only but within a few years they were building a six-wheeled, tractor-drawn, 85-foot aerial and a four-section 100-foot aerial ladder. Depending on the size of the ladder, customers would get a specific stabilization system to match. For a straight standard aerial up to 85 feet, customers would receive two hydraulic jacks that dropped straight down. For a straight standard aerial up to 100 feet, customers would receive the hydraulic outrigger jacks, or if the buyer chose another method, a swing-out screw-down style jack was also available. For a 100-foot tillered aerial, the swing-out screw-down jacks were used, but mounted closer to the turntable. All Maxim aerials were also equipped with a bull gear to assure smooth ladder rotation in all types of weather.

Also during the late 1940s, the Boston Fire Department engaged in a major apparatus replacement program that included purchasing equipment from Mack, Pirsch, FWD, Ward LaFrance and Maxim. Boston purchased two Maxim pumpers and two Maxim aerial ladders. One of the aerials went to the South Boston area and served as Ladder 21. It was a 65-foot aerial and rumor has it that it was ordered that way because there was a prison complex in its response area. Upon entering the prison complex, they had to pass completely through one gate, whereupon it would close behind them. When the first gate closed, the interior gate leading to the prison yard would open. The story has it that this was the only truck available with a total minimum length that would successfully fit in the enclosure. They also designed a new line of large crash rescue vehicles that didn't gain popularity until the early 1950s.

49

Overhead view of the Lexington truck shows the seat, with protection from the weather and access to the seat through the center of the hose bed.

This unfinished rig was headed to Medford, Oregon. West Coast departments often purchased Maxim chassis and were often finished by the George Heiser Body Company in Seattle, Washington.

At some point in the 1950s, Maxim decided to experiment again. Hoping to add a different model to the product line, the company introduced a line of fire trucks on International chassis, although, there was a slight change to the chassis—the International grille was removed and replaced with the trademark vertical Maxim grille. Called the Model VX, some of these unique looking rigs went to fire departments in North Reading, Massachusetts, South Royalton, Vermont and Cannon Corners, New York. This experiment was not successful, and there weren't many sold, but the VX model was available into the 1960s in varied forms. When asked about the design, one former Maxim employee remarked, "It was to make a dump truck look like a fire truck." The basic Maxim custom chassis remained the same but

Maxim introduced their all-metal aerial ladder in 1947. This aerial unit was built for Milton, Massachusetts. Photos of this particular aerial were often used in much of Maxim's ladder truck advertising.

A close-up view of the ladder sections that would become industry leaders. The ladder beams were two rolled sections coupled together to form a hollow I-beam design. This Maxim design didn't change much for almost 25 years.

To accomplish stability, Maxim used an "A" frame screw-down jacking system to be used on their aerial ladder trucks.

with a slight variation. A double front bumper was added with a larger bumper on the bottom and a slightly shorter one on top. This look would remain the same throughout most of the 1950s.

In 1951 Maxim experimented with its own rear-mounted aerial ladder truck. Luckily, a year later in 1952, Maxim acquired the rights to the Magirus aerial ladder of Germany with the hopes of building a prototype and demonstrating a new rear-mounted compact aerial ladder truck. The Magirus rear-mounted aerial ladder design was already successfully mounted on European fire trucks back in the 1930s. This new ladder truck was just slightly longer than a conventional Maxim

Top view of the turntable in the paint shop.

Bottom view of the same turntable assembly.

pumper. This new short wheelbase model carried a four-section 100-foot Magirus ladder. A 146-foot seven-section Magirus ladder was also available on the same chassis. The wheelbase on these models was a modest 203 inches. They were slow to catch on at first, but became the norm in the 1960s. They looked very bulky and, due to the turntable configuration, there was no feasible place to store ground ladders. The ladders that were stored there were removed before the turntable could rotate. However, they were far easier to maneuver in tight places. Philadelphia, Pennsylvania purchased the first one and soon after the design flaws were ironed out to make this particular model more "user-friendly." With a lifting capacity of up to 4,000 pounds it could also be used as a crane. This new rear-mounted aerial

ladder was clearly ahead of its time. The fire service did not realize its potential or start ordering these aerials in large numbers for another 14 years. Philadelphia, Pennsylvania purchased quite a few Maxims, as well as many other departments in the state of Pennsylvania. Most of these apparatus were sold through sales agent Fred Kauskrof from Oreland, Pennsylvania. Maxim also mounted some seven-section, 146-foot Maxim-Magirus rear-mounted aerials on seven Seagrave chassis for Green Bay, Wisconsin. In the 1960s, Maxim designed and offered a 170-foot Magirus aerial ladder as well as some 100-foot tillered aerials.

With the Maxim aerials becoming so popular, it would stand to reason why Indianapolis, Indiana would purchase a 1952 75-foot open cab aerial truck that

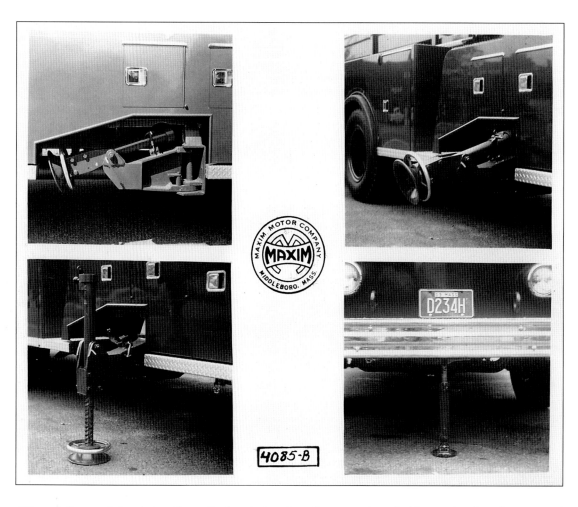

Although they are later photos, these display photos show the screw-down jacking system found on some of the Maxim aerials, including a jack in the front of the truck under the cab.

was assigned to Truck 18. This purchase would start a trend in Indianapolis, the former home of Stutz Fire Engine Company, that would make them a large buyer of Maxim equipment. They would go on to purchase 51 more pieces of apparatus over the next 17 years. A roster of apparatus for the Indianapolis department dated November 16, 1972, listed the following Maxim rigs in service: 34 pumpers, 6 aerials, 5 city service ladder trucks, 1 snorkel and 5 reserve pumps, for a grand total of 51 Maxim trucks in service at one time. The Indianapolis Fire Department also purchased several Maxim chassis and the department shops constructed five city service ladder trucks. Later in 1969 the Indianapolis Fire Department made a one-time purchase of 14 rigs with consecutive serial numbers beginning with 2732 and running through 2745. The Indianapolis department also took delivery of

Not many Maxim trucks made it out to Oklahoma, which was Boardman country, but Tulsa owned several Maxim aerials. One of them was this 1953 canopy cab 65-foot aerial with additional seating for the crew behind the cab.

This 1950s vintage aerial from Cranston, Rhode Island sported white-wall tires. Most aerial ladders came with a booster type pump and a very small water tank.

An excellent view of the distinctive Maxim front end on the Tulsa truck. Also note the "pompier," or scaling ladders, mounted on either side of the ladder.

In 1957, Owings Mills, Maryland purchased this 65-foot aerial quintuple combination with pump.

three 1,500-gpm Maxim pumpers in 1955, when the larger pumps of 1,250 to 1,500-gpm became available.

Despite Maxim's main market being in New England and the northeast, you could find Maxim fire trucks virtually all over the United States and beyond. Just some of the many sales agents that represented the Maxim company were:

•Gus Jacobs - White Plains, New York
•Richard Parkhurst – Dunellen, New Jersey
•John J. Duffy - Trenton, New Jersey, covering parts of New York, New Jersey and Pennsylvania

•Delta Fire & Safety Organization – New Orleans, Louisiana, covering Louisiana and Mississippi
•Butler Fire & Safety Company – Houston, Texas
•The Miami Fire Equipment Company – selling in southern Florida
•A. E. Hickerson of Central Fire Supply – Kansas

Even the West Coast had their share of agents in the Pacific Northwest and California. However, the company's largest market outside the northeast would remain in the heart of the Midwest in the state of Indiana. Maxims were also distributed

Maxim aerials were extremely popular with manufacturers that did not build their own ladders such as Mack. St. Louis, Missouri had this "B" model Mack with true open cab sent to Maxim for an 85-foot tillered trailer to be added.

through other Midwestern cities and towns by, appropriately enough, Midwest Fire & Safety Equipment in Indianapolis. One of their sales catalogs in 1961 remarked:

"Since January 1, 1948, Maxim is the preferred custom-built motor fire equipment line in the 30 largest cities in Indiana. These cities have purchased 83 pieces of Maxim apparatus consisting of 15 all-steel aerial ladder trucks, 60 pumping engines, two combination pumper-rescue squads, five city service ladder trucks and one quadruple combination."

This unbelievable record demonstrated that these cities received more Maxim appa-

ratus than all the other competitors in the area combined. Like with the Indianapolis department, Maxim occasionally supplied their Maxim chassis to other manufacturers like Young Fire Equipment Corporation of Buffalo, New York.

In 1953, Maxim's line of large airport crash trucks was finally recognized and sales rolled in. This heavy-duty crash rig was designed for civilian airports and built on a special off-road chassis supplied by the Walter Motor Company. Some of these trucks went to Washington D.C. and the New York Port Authority. The three rigs purchased by the New York Port Authority

Maxim offered a line of International chassis with a modified grille in the 1950s and 1960s called the Model VX. Bloomington, Indiana owned this 1957 model.

saw service at the Idlewild Airport (currently J. F. Kennedy International Airport), LaGuardia Airport in New York, and the Newark Airport in New Jersey. Maxim also supplied some smaller departments with smaller foam units on Maxim and commercial chassis also capable of foam output. Around the same time, Maxim closed down its automobile repair division to devote all of its efforts to the design, construction and manufacture of standard and commercial fire apparatus. Around this time, the plant was situated on a 4.8-acre site and contained a total of approximately 70,000 square feet that housed its design and staff facilities, three assembly areas, woodworking and machine shops, a sheet metal shop and a paint shop. These combined departments produced an annual sales volume as high as $1,500,000. The former automobile garage was used for the service, maintenance and repair of fire apparatus and the main plant was used for construction of new apparatus. Maxim products have been shipped to the far corners of the world including places such as Alaska, Greece, Japan, the Philippines, England and Central America including Brazil and Chile.

Duxbury, Massachusetts was another customer with a VX-75, 750-gpm pumper, also in 1957.

Maxim built more than just pumpers and aerials. Maxim built many forestry units starting in the 1930s. This mid-1950s Ford with front mount pump ran as Engine 4 in Rocky Hill, Connecticut.

Acquiring rights to the Magirus aerial ladder in 1952 allowed Maxim to produce a rear-mounted aerial on a smaller and more maneuverable frame. Philadelphia, Pennsylvania was the first department to purchase one and would eventually order several more over the years.

Rear view shows the screw-down jacks on the outside corners. The pair of bars on the inside is a lock-down device. The controls for the ladder itself are mounted on the left side of the turntable assembly.

This 100-foot Magirus tillered aerial was delivered to Newark, New Jersey in 1958. The photo of this truck was taken where most of the other Maxim factory photos were taken, at the Hannah Shaw Nursing Home just down the street from the Maxim factory. This rather upscale retirement home was the perfect backdrop for photos with almost 50 acres of manicured lawns and open landscape. Coincidentally, Hannah Shaw was a relative of Carlton Maxim and the Maxim family.

Many Maxim chassis were sold to other manufacturers. This truck, lettered for the Citizens Hose Company in Lancaster, New York, is thought to have bodywork by Young.

Advertising from *Fire Engineering* magazine dated April 1949 touts their line of large airport crash trucks on Walter chassis. The truck shown is described as a "Rescue Truck" built for the New York Port Authority to be used at the New York International Airport. A similar Maxim unit was stationed at nearby Newark Airfield in New Jersey.

A great view of a great looking Maxim! The Maxim grille had a very distinctive appearance that set it apart from other makes. This 1957 open cab pumper belonged to the Niantic Fire Department (Connecticut) in the East Lyme section of town. Engine 2 was a Model 2607 pumper complete with front suction intake and fender-mounted bell.

CHAPTER FIVE

BUSINESS AS USUAL

In 1956 the Seagrave Corporation of New York City purchased the Maxim Motor Company and control of the company was transferred from the Maxim family to the Seagrave Corporation. The name was changed from the Maxim Motor Company to the Maxim Motor Division. The Seagrave Corporation was the same company that built Seagrave fire apparatus.

With the change of owners came changes in titles. Ernest Maxim became Chairman of the Board; Joseph Whitcomb became President and Leighton Maxim became Vice President. The management of the company and the day-to-day operations continued as they did before with very little change. Maxim operated as the Maxim Motor Division, an independent division of Seagrave, and continued to manufacture all of its own apparatus and components including many styles of truck bodies and several models of ladders.

In 1957, Ernest Maxim passed away. He was considered one of the most prominent fire apparatus executives in the country. During his career he had served on several important committees that determined the future of the fire apparatus industry. He

served several terms as President of the Fire Apparatus Manufacturers Association as well as a member of several other important committees in the industry. The death of Leighton Maxim soon followed his fathers' just a few years later in 1961. Benjamin W. Lewis was chosen to fill the position of vice-president and Harold H. Hubbard was appointed clerk and treasurer. With most of the original founders passing away, many of the regular employees stepped up to fill the roles of management.

It is important to clarify here, and big business should take note, that the success of the company was also due to the loyalty of the employees and the pride expressed in their craftsmanship. Some employees remained with the company for nearly 50 years. Charles N. Warren, the first full-time employee hired by Carlton Maxim in 1899, was still with the company at the time of his death in 1958. Leon Perkins and William Winberg were other longtime employees both remaining with the company for the remainder of their careers. Charles (Bert) Carey, who came to the firm in 1915 to help, was still with the company in 1965. It wasn't unusual to have other employees

Springfield, Massachusetts was a large user of Maxim apparatus. This 1953 four-door rescue truck had plenty of compartment space. Springfield replaced this rescue unit with another Maxim S-Model four-door rescue about 20 years later.

This metalwork is a great example of Maxim's custom fabricating abilities and the craftsmanship of Maxim employees.

This 1955 Ford F-900, four-door pumper is believed to be the only four-door commercial chassis truck ever built by Maxim. It was delivered to Parkesburg, Pennsylvania in January 1956. It had a 750-gpm pump with 500-gallon tank and a cab that held six people. It served a second life in New Hampshire for several years before being sold to a collector. It was eventually restored and is now privately owned.

complete a 25-year or longer tenure with the firm. As one former employee admitted, "the pay was average, but the administration more than made up for it with caring and compassion." Another former employee made mention that taking time off for family business was never an issue. In one specific case, where transportation was a concern, management was always there with the company car to provide transportation to and from.

Over the years Maxim would face competition from other fire apparatus manufacturers in Massachusetts. There was Continental in Hopkinton, Farrar in Woodville and Maynard from Marshfield. Other smaller New England companies came and went over the years such as E. G. Moody, Gibson, Middlesex, Moore, Robinson, Wood and Zabek but none could gain an edge over a company that already had a firm foothold on the region. The business

One of many exports from Maxim was this aerial ladder that was sent overseas to Korea. This was an X50QLA65 aerial. Breaking down the model number is quite easy once you learn how. The "X50" was a standard commercial package, the "Q" stood for quint, "LA" for ladder and "65" was simply the length of the aerial. The interesting part of this truck is the MEMCO ladder—highly unusual for a company known for their own brand of aerials.

continued to grow even larger and the sales area expanded immensely extending into the export market. In 1958 a newspaper photo appeared in a New England newspaper showing four Maxim fire trucks being loaded onto a freighter heading to South Korea. These fully equipped rigs were built on REO chassis and had 300-gallon water tanks with 500-gpm pumps. Another interesting export that may have been part of the same order was a rear-mounted aerial ladder quintuple combination (or quint) designed and built for a department in Korea on what appeared to be an International chassis. This Model X50QLA85 was a rare truck indeed as it had a MEMCO ladder. For a company known exclusively for its own aerial ladders, Carlton would have surely rolled over in his grave if he knew this ladder was to be mounted on

Maxim introduced its first cab forward F-Model pumper in October 1958. The very first cab forward model produced was delivered to the South Bend Fire Department in Indiana. This sales advertisement dated February 1959 announces Maxim's newest product.

a Maxim truck. The model numbers were quite simple to translate: the "X-50" denotes a commercial chassis with standard pump package with a 500-gpm pump. The "Q" stood for quint, and the "LA85" denoted a ladder with an 85-foot length. A Model X-75 was a commercial chassis with a 750-gpm pump.

After being absorbed by Seagrave, some new ideas and new perspectives

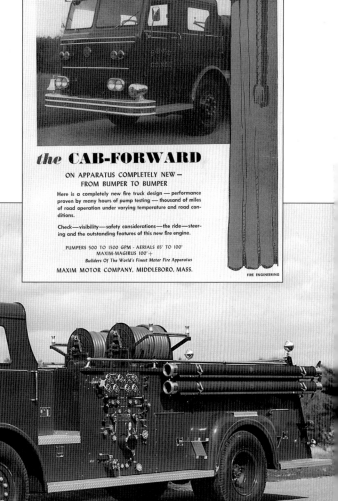

MAXIM

Announces —

the CAB-FORWARD

ON APPARATUS COMPLETELY NEW — FROM BUMPER TO BUMPER

Here is a completely new fire truck design — performance proven by many hours of pump testing — thousand of miles of road operation under varying temperature and road conditions.

Check — visibility — safety considerations — the ride — steering and the outstanding features of this new fire engine.

PUMPERS 500 TO 1500 GPM - AERIALS 65' TO 100'
MAXIM-MAGIRUS 100'+
Builders Of The World's Finest Motor Fire Apparatus

MAXIM MOTOR COMPANY, MIDDLEBORO, MASS.

FIRE ENGINEERING

This factory photo of the South Bend pumper shows the early cab forward design before it was slightly modified and refined a bit.

Front view of the typical F-Model cab forward.

brought invigorating changes in 1959 with the introduction of the "F" series cab forward and also in 1960 with the introduction of the "S" series short wheelbase. The "F" series, or cab forward design, was available with either open or closed cab and seating for five passengers. Shortly afterward, the "S" series, or the engine forward, was introduced. These two designs complimented each other nicely giving a prospective customer two distinct choices to choose from. The S-Model was designed to look squarer than its predecessor, the conventional Maxim apparatus that everyone had known and loved during the 1940s and 1950s. It boasted a rather boxy

Front view of the S-Model short wheelbase engine-ahead-of-cab pumper, complete with bell, Federal Q siren and canvas top.

A Maxim advertisement from *Fire Engineering* magazine dated October 1960 announces the arrival of the new S-Model and all the advantages over a cab forward design. These two choices complimented each other nicely giving prospective buyers two distinct choices of apparatus.

look with a square nose, flat-faced radiator, quad headlights and a wraparound bumper that was flush across the front with the corners wrapping around to the front of the fenders. One unique S-Model was delivered to the Weavertown Fire Department in Lebanon Township, Pennsylvania. It was an open cab pumper with a white and blue paint scheme, dubbed "Blue Max." Some other features that made the S-Model desirable over the cab forward models were its shorter overall length and

shorter turning radius, even though they had identical wheelbases and components. The "F" and "S" series were available for both pumpers and aerials and could be ordered with either gasoline engines by Waukesha or diesel engines by Cummins or Detroit. The diesel engines were available as either a 6-cylinder engine with 240 or 265 available horsepower or an 8-cylinder of 320 available horsepower. At this point in time, Maxim pumpers came with Hale pumps that were considered top of the line. Customers also had a choice of pumps ranging from 500-gpm to 2,000-gpm and booster tanks ranging in capacities from 300 gallons to 1,000 gallons of water. The aerials were available in a straight job or tractor-trailer type with aerial sizes going up to 100 feet in length. The Maxim logo on the front of the vehicles also changed slightly with the introduction of the "F" series. The "F" series sported a larger logo, approximately

continued on page 75

Washington, Indiana took delivery of this 1959 Model F26110 closed cab pumper. Note the full length and full width doors.

This Model F262LA85, serial number 2317, served in Albertson, New York. It's now privately owned. The "262" in the model designation denotes a gas engine.

A slight variation on the cab forward model was this cab forward pumper built for East Gary, Indiana. This Model CFX75 was an experimental truck built on an International bus chassis in 1959. Notice the full-length door and how wide the cab was in relation to the standard F-Model cab.

The same truck viewed from the right side shows how the wider cab allowed for a sideward style seating arrangement to the rear of the cab instead of the usual rear-facing seats. A similar open cab pumper of this design was delivered to Terre Haute, Indiana.

Another of these unique units was delivered to the Connersville, Indiana department in 1959. This FXQLA75 had a 75-foot aerial, 750-gpm pump and a 150-gallon tank. This style is very reminiscent of the earlier American LaFrance JOX type chassis.

Many of the volunteer departments on Long Island took great pride in their apparatus. Croton-On-Hudson, New York was no exception. This was a 1963 Model F26210C. The "C" in the model designation meant that this truck had compartments along the body.

6 inches wide, quite a bit larger than the standard enameled version. They were cast in brass by the Colonial Brass Company of Taunton and plated with chrome. They were then painted red and white. The "S" series remained the same for a few more years, using the smaller emblem on the front of the nose above the radiator, but was eventually adorned with the same large emblem as the F-Model around 1968. Surprisingly, the conventional Maxim chassis were still available but fading away to the

newer models. Their appearance changed slightly with a single front bumper and a change to quad headlights instead of the single teardrop-style headlight.

The 1960s saw many changes in the way of design and materials being used in fire apparatus. Plastics were being used in the interiors and fiberglass and aluminum were being used to reduce weight. Automatic transmissions were becoming even more popular, as were diesel engines. V-8 engines and air suspension systems

Bench seating along the top and boot racks were not normal features on a standard apparatus but added some nice touches.

made their debut. Gas turbine engines also made a brief appearance before proving that much maintenance was required to maintain them.

In 1963 the company changed hands again when FWD (Four Wheel Drive Auto Company) purchased the Seagrave Corporation. The Seagrave Corporation then became known as the Seagrave Fire Apparatus Division, and Maxim continued to operate under their separate and original name given under Seagrave—the Maxim Motor Division. FWD continued to focus their efforts on the manufacture of rough terrain vehicles while Maxim continued selling their wares wherever possible. Maxim worked hard to maintain a large network of sales agents all over the United States. Another little hot spot of Maxim apparatus was the Long Island area of New York. Many of the volunteer departments that held a great deal of pride in

The chrome pump panel and additional gold leafing on the compartment doors added a finishing touch!

their apparatus chose Maxim to reflect that sense of pride. The sales agent in the New York area mostly responsible for this popularity was the Superior Coach & Equipment Company of Rochester, New York. In addition to Maxim apparatus the sales agent dealt in Superior Ambulances as the name implied.

A few years later, in 1966, Crown Coach of Los Angeles added tractor-drawn and service aerials to their product line. As mentioned earlier, the Maxim Motor Division supplied these aerials. Some of these Crown Coach/Maxim aerials could be seen in the TV series Emergency, a popular show during the 1970s. Crown Coach did not manufacture aerial ladders and had to rely on Maxim aerials for their products. It is believed that all Crown Coach aerials were built with Maxim ladders. In comparison with other fire apparatus manufacturers, Crown did not make many ladder trucks.

The S-Model pumper was a favorite of many departments. This Model S26210 pumper was ordered by Indianapolis, Indiana in 1965. Indianapolis was the largest user of Maxim apparatus outside of New England.

In all, there were 30 Crown/Maxim rigs, 10 tractor-drawn tillers (8 100-foot ladders and 2 75-foot ladders), 7 mid-mount aerials (all 100 feet in length) and 13 rear-mount aerials (all 100 feet in length).

In 1967 Joseph Whitcomb retired as Chairman of the Maxim Motor Division. Shortly thereafter, the S-Model changed by making the cab slightly wider. A new addition to the aerial ladder line was the introduction of the Top-Trol device. The Top-Trol device is a control that allowed the firefighter positioned at the top of

the ladder full control to rotate, elevate or lower the ladder using a control box at the tip of the fly section. The operator on the turntable could override the Top-Trol when needed. Also around this time Maxim began building elevating platforms, or snorkels, using Pitman platform booms. Larger models had to be built on rigs with tandem rear ends to distribute the weight. They also delivered chassis, mostly F-Models, to Pierce for use in constructing snorkels. One of these snorkels saw service in South Euclid, Ohio. It was

Another 1965 Maxim was this Model S26210C canopy cab pumper delivered to Worcester, Massachusetts.

a Maxim chassis that was sent to Pierce for the bodywork. It was equipped with a 1,250-gpm pump and an 85-foot Pitman snorkel. However, the snorkel was compatible with either the "F" or "S" chassis. Another unusual rig was an 85-foot snorkel that was delivered to Gary, Indiana. The unusual feature was that this was an S-Model truck. The middle of the boom extended out over the front of the truck quite far—almost the length of the truck itself—giving the impression the truck would tip over forward.

The late 1960s found Maxim still at the top of the fire truck industry ranked as the number 2 custom builder. Then Vice-President and sales manager Ben Lewis reported that the national annual fire truck production rate for 1967 was about 2,500 units with Maxim producing approximately 100 trucks a year. They still managed to please customers with personal service and commitment by providing the best equipment and parts at the most reasonable prices. A local New Bedford newspaper, *The Standard Times*, featured a story on

Philadelphia, Pennsylvania was a valued customer of Maxim and took delivery of this mid 1960s S262LAT100 tillered aerial.

Maxim in February 1967 and remarked, "Walking through Maxim's plant suggests the mournful eulogies often voiced for Yankee craftsmanship are decidedly premature. It is Yankee craftsmanship welded to top-drawer engineering and the best of materials that have won Maxim its good name." The feature story went on to describe how the construction process of building a truck begins with the needs of the department reflected in the engineering and then out to the factory where the materials are assembled with the greatest of care. The finishing touches include the chrome, shiny paint and pride. At the time of the article, the fire truck receiving its paint was a Kelly-green colored pumper being built for the Hibernian Engine Company, a group of volunteers in New Jersey. When the eight prime coats and four paint coats had cured, the truck received its gold-leafed shamrock on the doors.

A small windshield is all that protected the tiller man on the rear of the trailer.

Saylesville, Rhode Island owned this 1964 Mack with a 75-foot Maxim aerial.

This photo from the 1970s shows a Maxim aerial doing what it did best—fighting fire. This aerial was on the job in Springfield, Massachusetts. *Photo by Don Fontaine, courtesy of David Deane Collection*

This white Model S2627C protected Portsmouth, Rhode Island.

Rutland, Vermont owned this Model S2627Q quadruple combination. The box mounted just behind the cab carries a life net.

Brattleboro, in southern Vermont, used this 1965 four-door Model S26210C. Many departments in New England liked the four-door trucks because they kept crews out of the weather. Other Vermont departments with four-door Maxim pumpers included Barnard, Enosburg Falls and Rutland.

The Bureau of Fire in Wilmington, Delaware ran this 1966 Model S262R as a rescue and lighting unit.

Shop Order #F-413 was this unfinished Maxim F-Model that appears to be destined to become a snorkel with the wide-bodied, flotation type rear tires. However, Maxim records indicate this Model F26210SQ75 cab and chassis was actually to become a quint aerial ladder destined for Bellevue, Kentucky. This chassis was frequently used for Maxim-Pierce-built snorkels.

Marion, Massachusetts took delivery of this Model X-20 brushbreaker in 1964. Maxim built many of these forestry units for nearby departments but did not design them. Local departments in the Cape Cod area started building their own brushbreakers in the 1930s. Other Massachusetts builders like Farrar also built similar rigs.

CHAPTER SIX

SEASONS OF CHANGE

In the early 1970s Maxim introduced another line of new products. They included a variety of specialized bodies on commercial and custom chassis. According to a sales brochure at the time, "MAXIM offers the equipment that's right for the job—pumpers, floodlight and rescue units, aerials, tank wagons, pumps of almost any capacity. Large hose bodies, special compartmentation, foam systems, front and rear suction inlets and high-pressure pumps. These are just a few of the typical MAXIM apparatus and installations available with Cummins diesel power plants." The Cummins diesels were available in three sizes, 240 horsepower, 265 horsepower and 320 horsepower, commonly coupled with an Allison automatic transmission, or a Fuller or Spicer synchromesh standard transmission. A few years later, Detroit Diesels were also made available leaving the customer with more options. Waukesha gas engines were still available but were becoming less desirable in lieu of the more economical diesels.

One specialty vehicle excluded in the sales literature was a forest fire truck, commonly referred to as a "brushbreaker" throughout New England. The brushbreakers were unique vehicles that were

specifically designed to fight forest fires in the Cape Cod area. They were built on a 4 x 4 chassis with tank water and a pump-and-roll capability. They had heavy iron bars wrapped around the front, sides and rear of the vehicle, and these bars were used to actually push over small to medium sized trees in an attempt to gain access to fires deep in the woods. Maxim did not design these brushbreakers. They had been department-built by many local fire departments going back as far as the early 1930s. The earliest brushbreakers were nothing more than four-wheel drive trucks with extra protection (extra bumpers) on the fronts of the vehicles. However, Maxim did have their own model to sell to departments unable to produce their own. They also built smaller brush units on pickup truck chassis.

Another unique vehicle Maxim offered was called the "Mini-Max." The "Mini-Max" was a small golf cart sized vehicle approximately 11 feet long, 4 feet wide and 6 feet tall. It weighed approximately 2,800 pounds. It was primarily designed for areas such as shopping malls, parking garages, schools, colleges, factories, warehouses, and convention halls and sports stadiums. It could carry an array of tools

Other specialty vehicles included smaller forestry units like this Model X-10 built for the Wareham Forest Fire Department using a four-wheel-drive 1966 Dodge Power Wagon W-300. It had a 250-gpm portable pump and a 250-gallon tank.

and equipment. One model could carry as much as one 150-pound dry chemical unit, one 20-pound dry chemical extinguisher, one 2 1/2-gallon pressurized water extinguisher, one 2-section 12-foot extension ladder, two fire axes and a mounted SCBA unit. The "Mini-Max" also came with up to six compartments for smaller hand tools. Another option was the availability of remote control. It could self-start; lights and siren activate and deliver itself to 40 pre-determined locations within the complex without a driver. A safety bumper would stop the vehicle at any obstruction and an audible horn would sound until the obstruction was moved. It would then continue on its way to its destination. Once there, a driver could move the unit to any other location.

At least two of these unusual units were sold, with one going to The Bruedan Corporation, a manufacturer of golf carts. It's unclear if this unique vehicle was based on one of their units, or if the competition

A 1965 Ford "C" cab pumper built for Nantucket, Massachusetts on an all-wheel drive chassis. The pump was mounted in the rear to accommodate the all-wheel-drive equipment and the short wheelbase helped navigate the narrow roads in that seaside community.

was looking for an edge. The buildings and grounds remained pretty much the same with little or no changes. Production continued as usual, the truck frames would be brought into the main building and run along in an assembly line fashion where the drive train, pump, and plumbing were equipped. It's important to note that we compare the construction to an assembly line. However, Maxim did not use an assembly line and the appropriate term was "stall-building." Because of the

uniqueness of custom-built trucks, an assembly line was not practical. Four to five employees would start the truck and move it along to another shop where more work was completed, and so on. Next, the truck was sent to the body shop and paint booth (also called "the Dog Patch" by employees), where the bodywork and paint would be added along with extras like chrome trim, stainless steel and pump gauges. The trucks were then pump tested and road tested. Many Maxim employees were

One innovative yet short-lived Maxim product was the Mini-Max shown in this Maxim sales literature. The Mini-Max was a golf cart sized apparatus that could carry fire equipment, via remote control, throughout areas where access by fire truck was too difficult such as at shopping malls, warehouses, factories and parking garages. At least two were sold in the 1970s, with one going to the Bruedan Corporation.

firefighters in local communities. It should be understood that firefighters have an unusual sense of adventure and humor. One amusing story has it from a former employee that he was scolded for something that he did test-driving a tillered aerial. Most of us know that a good tiller man can get the trailer to swing out next to the cab. One day during a test drive, the tiller man swung the trailer out next to the cab to say hello to the driver of the

apparatus and management caught him. The moral of the story was—let it be known that this is not recommended on a brand new apparatus on its virgin run. Another remarkable story has it that a fire chief had come down to see how progress was coming on a pumper that was ordered. As luck would have it, it was going to be road tested that very day. Since non-employees were not allowed to ride the apparatus for liability reasons, the chief was allowed to follow along behind in his personal vehicle during the test run. During the road test, the truck (for unknown reasons) ran off the road and into a sturdy old oak tree which totaled the truck. Luckily nobody was injured, but the chief sure had a story to tell when he returned to the department that afternoon. Many a story like this was heard from some of the former employees.

Maxim had introduced a line of the modified International VX model pumpers back in the 1950s that remained available up into the 1960s. Maxim continued using the International chassis for another new model of apparatus that featured a front mount pump. The front mounted pumps were advantageous for some departments who required lots of drafting from static water sources. If access allowed, the trucks could drive right down to the water's edge and put the pump right to the edge of the water, decreasing the lift on the draft. Mostly found in rural settings, some of these trucks went to Marlow, New Hampshire; Goodwin's Mills, Maine; and Middles Falls, New York.

However, probably one of the most unique apparatus ever built by Maxim was delivered to the Massachusetts Port Authority to protect the Logan International Airport in Boston, Massachusetts. It was a yellow 1971 Maxim F-Model (cab forward) with a V-8 Cummins diesel engine. It carried

Other than drive trains and pumps, Maxim's custom apparatus was scratch built from the frame up. The chassis was constructed, the pump was added and the body was installed.

Shop Order #F-272 - Taken against a snowy, New England backdrop, this photo shows a 1964 X-50 pumper with 500-gpm front mount pump. This truck belonged to North Brookfield, Massachusetts and ran as Engine 3. With just the red nose and front fender, could this still be called a white-over-red paint job?

1,000 gallons of water, had a 1,000-gpm pump with pump-and-roll capability, a 220-gallon foam bladder tank (it was situated inside the water tank itself) and two 500-pound tanks of a dry chemical agent (Purple K) that were discharged via two nitrogen cylinders. Other equipment included a Lockwood manual turret on the roof, two under-the-truck nozzles to protect the undercarriage, and four 100-foot booster lines, two of which discharged foam and the other two that discharged dry chemical agent. According to a deputy chief at the airport, the truck drove fine around the relatively flat grades inside the airport complex. However, if the truck left the airport to respond to mutual aid calls, it had quite a time climbing many of the hills in the Boston area fully loaded with water and equipment, which it did when it responded to the Chelsea conflagration in October 1973.

Foam pumpers were not sold to airports alone. Other departments in proximity to smaller airfields or major highways purchased Maxim pumpers

A close-up view of the front mount pump. Rural fire departments with limited water supplies often had to draft from static sources like rivers, ponds and lakes. Front mount pumps were preferred on their apparatus so that the trucks could be driven down to the water's edge to create a more effective drafting operation.

with foam capability. The main foam turret was located on the roof, with the option of several under-carriage nozzles under the front bumper. Since these trucks also had a pump-and-roll capability, the driver had to increase the throttle in the cab, all the while standing on the brake with both feet to keep the truck from crawling away. Some operators even reported using this foam turret with straight water as a deck gun to darken down a heavy fire condition while master streams were being set up. In the mid 1970s the S-Model changed again slightly.

The front engine compartment increased in size to accommodate a larger engine. The grille got wider with chrome trim vertically down the left and right sides of the radiator with a similar chrome strip vertically down the center. The bumper was also straight across the front of the vehicle and the windshield was made larger. One of these newer S-Model Maxims went to Clinton, Maryland, a department that prided itself on its deluxe taste in fire apparatus. This particular truck was an open cab S-Model painted a patriotic red, white and blue. It also sported a rear

Attleboro, Massachusetts took delivery of this foam pumper Model F26210C with Rockwood foam system. Maxim offered several types of engines with their custom apparatus. Gasoline engines were supplied by Waukesha, and Cummins or Detroit supplied the diesel counterparts. The diesel engines were available in 240 or 265 horsepower 6-cylinder engines or a 320 horsepower 8-cylinder engine. A firefighter who drove a similar truck reported that these foam trucks were so high powered that drivers had to keep the brake pedal depressed with both feet to keep the truck stationary while the engine worked away supplying foam!

windshield for the crew riding the rear step. This rear windshield was originally designed for riot protection during the years of civil unrest, but it was also used on some rigs to provide road debris protection for firefighters riding the back step. Unfortunately, word has it that this great looking rig didn't last long and was destroyed in a rollover accident in the 1980s.

Another unfortunate accident involving Maxim fire apparatus occurred in the early 1970s, but this one had disastrous consequences. On June 17, 1972, Boston firefighters responded to 160 Commonwealth Avenue for a fire in the Hotel Vendome. Four alarms were struck to bring this stubborn fire under control and within a few hours the fire was

Maxim built this large crash truck for Pratt & Whitney in 1963. Pratt & Whitney produced aircraft engines in Hartford, Connecticut. It is believed that this truck, a Model F26210K, was a large nurse tanker built on a Walter 6 x 6 chassis with Maxim bodywork. It had a 1,000-gpm rear-mount pump and a 2,500-gallon water tank. A Rockwood foam roof turret was added later. The gentleman standing in the photo was longtime Maxim employee and engineer, Earl Everhardt. *Photo courtesy of Garry Santaniello*

out and companies were in the building overhauling. Suddenly, without warning, the corner of the building on Dartmouth Street collapsed, burying many firefighters. Nine firefighters were injured and nine others paid the supreme sacrifice. Also under the rubble lay Ladder 15, a 1971 Maxim "F" cab, 100-foot tillered aerial. When the firefighters were removed, work began on digging out the aerial. When uncovered, it was found still running. The

ladder section and trailer were completely destroyed in the collapse; however, the cab was salvaged and later paired with a Seagrave ladder to be used as a reserve piece. A few months later, Boston Fire Department received a replacement, a 1973 Maxim "F" 100-foot tillered aerial.

On an encouraging and more upbeat note, Maxim was still enjoying a positive reputation and business was as steady as ever—for the time being.

In 1965 Nanuet, New York took delivery of this F52R rescue and lighting unit. There are a total of 9 "Circle-D" lights atop the body. This truck was used in sales advertising for Circle-D.

New Hyde Park, New York operated this 1968 Model F26215C pumper with rear windshield and additional warning lights on the front end.

In the late 1970s, Trenton, New Jersey purchased these identical lime-yellow pumpers. Lime yellow was a trend in the 1970s when it was believed that it was more visible than red or white.

CHAPTER SEVEN

FINANCIAL WOES

In the mid-to-late 1970s, Maxim's parent company, Seagrave, opened a new branch in Ontario, Canada that failed miserably and weakened the company. For a very brief time, even Maxim commercial fire apparatus were built in this Canadian facility. However, it was soon recognized that most of the apparatus constructed at this plant were so poorly constructed that before the units were sold, they had to be brought to the Middleboro facility to be repaired due to poor workmanship and corrected before being delivered to the customers. During this time, inflation and a lack of sales deeply affected all major fire apparatus manufacturers including giants like American LaFrance, Mack and Ward LaFrance. Seagrave decided to focus its attention on improving their own products and protecting their investments. In 1975 the Seagrave Corporation sold Maxim to North Street Associates of Greenwich, Connecticut, a pair of investors who also owned Ward LaFrance and Ward LaFrance International in Elmira, New York. The principal partners in North Street Associates were Charles E. Bradley and David P.

Agnew. The pair changed the name from the Maxim Motor Division to Maxim Industries. Wilbur R. (Buzz) Oakley, a current Maxim employee, took over as President of the company in 1973 and oversaw the transition. Buzz Oakley had started with the company in 1967.

Production for the company from 1975 through 1978 averaged about ten trucks a month; typically eight pumpers and two aerial ladders. Maxim also guaranteed a custom apparatus from stock in one week or less.

Shortly after the transition, Maxim Industries began to experience some financial difficulties, most likely associated with the national recession and local economy, or a combination of the two. Many employees felt the new owners had no experience and no business being in the fire truck business and as investors had made many poor decisions regarding the business. To cope with the financial problems, they applied for and received a loan in the amount of $900,000 from the Middleborough Trust Company. The Maxim firm had never been in a more

Another late 1970s pumper was ordered by Willowick, Ohio. Willowick also owned a one-of-a-kind Maxim closed cab, closed body city service aerial back in the 1950s.

vulnerable position. A newspaper article featured in the Boston Globe on January 3, 1976, brought these financial woes into the public arena. Apparently four Massachusetts cities, Arlington, Salem, Somerville and Wakefield, had signed contracts with Maxim Industries for new apparatus. The company, hit by a shortage of supplies and materials coupled with the spiraling costs of engine accessories, tried to pass this price increase on to its customers. However, the cities weren't buying it and they took Maxim to court. Desperately in need of their new apparatus, Arlington, Salem and Wakefield settled out of court for slightly higher than their original contracts. Somerville was successful in getting an injunction against Maxim. The

court order prevented Maxim from selling three inferior fire trucks it had offered the city, in lieu of the three originally ordered, until the original three arrived. The cities' strategy had worked. Maxim agreed, out of court, to provide the three original pieces by a certain date for the original prices, or face a $50-a-day fine for every day beyond the deadline. Inflation and the nation's economy were indeed taking their toll on everyone and this was not the Maxim that everyone had been accustomed to doing business with.

With the new name came more changes for the apparatus model line. Maxim Industries still offered the F- and S-Model chassis, but they gained new nicknames in the marketing world. The F-Model cab forward chassis was labeled the "Marauder" and the "S" engine ahead-of-cab-chassis was dubbed the "Yankee." Maxim Industries also produced a commercial chassis labeled the "Blazer."

As mentioned earlier, North Street Associates also owned Ward LaFrance International of Elmira, New York. Although owned by the same parent company, Maxim and Ward LaFrance technically continued to operate independently of one another, producing their own brands of apparatus. Literature on the company at the time listed the marketing office of Maxim Industries as being in Elmira, New York and the factory office in Middleboro, Massachusetts. However, there was some convenient sharing of resources that went along with this cooperative merger. Both Ward LaFrance and Maxim pumpers shared some common identifiers such as the cab style and teardrop-shaped window on the F-Model chassis. The trademark window could be found on the side of the truck between the standard jump seat window and the cab doors. Some time ago, Maxim started purchasing cabs from Truck Cab Manufacturers, Inc., of Cincinnati, Ohio. These cabs were commonly referred to simply as "Cincinnati cabs." They also offered three distinct styles of the cab forward cab: the Maxim II Full-Vision (the standard Maxim cab); the Maxim IV – Maxi-Vision (which looked identical to the Ward LaFrance Ultra-Vision cab with trademark windshield); and the Maxim III – Panoramic-Vision (which was a wraparound type that resembled a Young Crusader). Records indicate only a handful of Maxim III cabs that can positively be confirmed to have existed. Prince Frederick Volunteer Fire Department in Calvert County, Maryland owned one as well as a business in Odessa, Texas, and a department on Long Island, New York.

Many of the customers weren't happy and in some cases declined Maxim's business when it was learned that most of the Maxim pumpers were built in the Ward LaFrance plant in New York, and all the aerial ladders, regardless of make, were built in Middleboro. One source reports that due to friction between the employees and management, that management moved the pumper production to Elmira in an attempt to weaken the employee's union. Regardless of cause, this move alone reduced the work force from 200 employees working three shifts to 100 employees working one shift. The move also resulted in a lack of orders, which started to seriously affect the cash flow of the company. The reduction in the amount of pumpers being built in the Middleboro factory also affected the number of workers needed. This led to even more layoffs of the skilled workers at the Ward LaFrance plant and eventually to lower profits. The employees could see the writing on the wall. Many of the faithful and longtime original Maxim employees left the company for other employment. Talks of additional layoffs, financial insecurity and the inability to cash payroll checks were not positive signs to the workers. Yet the company insisted on hiring more employees while production and workload decreased. The union had asked on several occasions for additional layoffs to whittle down the workforce to a manageable level but was unsuccessful.

On December 31, 1978, the Ward LaFrance factory in Elmira was forced to close down due to an increase in labor and material costs and the unbearable competition from larger fire apparatus manufacturers such as Pierce and Emergency One. It was in the cards that smaller manufacturers were in for the fight of their lives. Many of the Ward LaFrance orders that went unfinished were sent to Maxim to

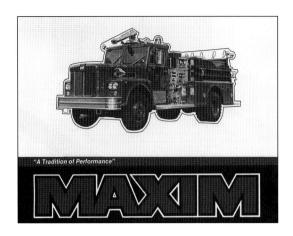

"A Tradition of Performance"

An example of Maxim sales literature from the early 1980s. This one-page advertisement with photo on the front and specifications on the back shows an S-Model pumper lettered for Springfield, Massachusetts. Maxim offered three chassis and styles. The S-Model was dubbed the "Yankee," the F-Model was the "Marauder," and the commercial chassis carried the name "Blazer."

be completed. North Street Associates also sent many of the laid off workers from the Ward factory to work in Middleboro, where they were put up in hotels.

When a Ward dealer won a bid for an aerial, it was a Maxim aerial on a Ward chassis. When orders arrived, work began immediately. Construction began on a contract for several 100-foot rear-mounted aerial ladders for the United States Navy to be distributed throughout the United States. Maxim continued using Cincinnati cabs on their apparatus. In comparison to the older style cabs, these newer cabs overall were wider with narrow type fenders. Production time on these units varied depending on materials needed and the sizes of the vehicles. An average sized pumper would take about 30 days to build while an aerial ladder would take twice that at 60 days. The union workers that comprised

the work force consisted of every trade imaginable such as welders, burners, machinists, cutters, electricians, mechanics, pipe fitters, metal fabricators and even a person who designed and painted the gold leaf trim and lettering, namely Robert Schofield of Middleboro.

In 1981, Maxim celebrated its 67th birthday. However, misfortunes continued to plague the company—inventory was disappearing, material and stock supplies dwindled, health insurance benefits were cut, and little work was coming in. One day in January two workers were delivering a fire truck to Providence where an agent of the Internal Revenue Service met them. He informed them that he was the new owner of that truck, that Maxim had not paid its payroll taxes in several years. Owing at least $500,000 in employee withholdings and even more on the original loan, the end had finally arrived.

With its capital gone, and still under obligation to the Middleborough Trust for the $900,000 loan, Maxim was forced to lay off 100 employees and padlock the doors on January 26, 1981. Without capital they could no longer finance parts or payroll. Maxim Industries became involved in Chapter 11 proceedings. The bank assumed control of the company. With many financial troubles and criminal suits being filed against part of the management, it appeared that Maxim was going to suffer the same fate as Ward LaFrance had under the same ownership. North Street Associates became the subject of an FBI inquiry investigating whether the owners had skimmed profits and deliberately caused high debt only to knowingly file for bankruptcy. Many of the former employees harbored ill will towards the ownership believing that they purchased the company as an investment with the intentions of bleeding it dry of its assets. With two popular and successful fire apparatus manufacturers out of the business, this would appear to be correct. It is important to note that the FBI investigation found no evidence of misconduct on the part of the ownership.

One of the Maxim employees came forward in October 1981 in an attempt to rescue the ailing company, determined to breathe new life into the Maxim organization. The bank sold the assets of the company, totaling some $720,000, to David G. Deane and two other participants, brothers Joseph and Gary Castanino. David Deane, who would be the principal impetus for the re-birth of the company, was a 39-year veteran of the company and a fire apparatus equipment supplier of his own in Springfield, Massachusetts.

Deane was a former newspaper reporter in Springfield, Massachusetts and was fascinated with the fire service. He took the civil service examination but was never hired as a firefighter, although during World War II Deane was a member of the firefighting crew in the Navy at the Brooklyn Navy base. After his discharge from the service in 1947, he started working for Maxim as a salesman and an authorized Maxim dealer in western Massachusetts, New York and Vermont. He was also the longtime owner of Deane Fire Equipment Company Incorporated in Springfield. Sharing time between the two companies proved his dedication to making things work for the ailing Maxim company. To manage operations Deane commuted. He made the long trip to Middleboro from Springfield and stayed in Middleboro for a few days before returning to Springfield for the rest of the week.

He resumed control of the company on November 2, 1981, changed the name of the company to Maxim Motor Company Incorporated, immediately re-hired 55 of the 100 former employees, and began

Other 1980s advertising shows this example of an F-Model cab forward "Marauder" in aerial form.

preparing bids for new apparatus. Within three months, the Castanino brothers were out of the picture leaving David Deane to try to manage the company on his own. Despite some economic stresses such as high labor costs and shrinking municipal budgets, the company began a rapid recovery during a time when the economy was on shaky ground. Other businesses in Massachusetts were seriously affected by proposition 2 1/2, a local tax-cutting measure that cut state aid to most communities. Part of Deane's success was due to the minor but very important details of the proposition. He knew a great many fire chiefs in the area, due to his past sales experiences, and the staff was extremely sure to attend important seminars, meetings and conventions that dealt with fire apparatus manufacturing. Another successful tactic was the versatility of the employees. Many employees would take on dual responsibilities and roles. For instance, Tom Reis the Vice-President and General Manager served as a production manager and apparatus tester. Another employee, Sales Manager Bill Pizura also served as a

Colts Neck, New Jersey owned this massive 1973 1,000-gpm pumper tanker with a 1,000-gallon booster tank with tandem rear end. The S-Model engine compartment was enlarged during the 1970s to accommodate the larger engines. The chrome trim was standard on these new grilles. *Photo courtesy of Dick Adelman Collection*

purchasing agent. Dale Lawrence served as the company secretary, office manager and company historian. Like the past, the company was able to build the entire vehicle, except for the motor and transmission, allowing them to assemble the apparatus to suit any specific needs of the purchasing community. In the mid 1980s they were able to produce three trucks a month with a six- to eight-month lead-time. When Deane took over the company there were over a dozen unfilled orders on the books from the previous company for new apparatus. Without obligation, Maxim Motor Company Incorporated assumed those new orders despite the fact that they would

lose money on them initially. It was a positive for the new company since there were no new orders during the start-up to prove that the company had a credible and capable position in the marketplace, as well as good will towards the communities hoping for new apparatus. The new company took a financial hit on the new work since they were constructed in 1981 using the original 1979-1980 contracts. Those orders were quickly completed while the staff went on a sales trip to search out new business. In their first year, they sold 23 rigs to 20 customers, a far cry from the volume the company was used to after World War II, when 150 workers could produce six to

Nahant, Massachusetts owned this 1979 100-foot rear mount aerial with white-over-red paint job. The teardrop style window between the driver's door and jump seat window is one of the common denominators of the Maxim-Ward LaFrance trucks of this era. *Photo courtesy of Rich Louf*

seven trucks a month. Within the next few years the company would double its business annually and eventually try to maintain a healthy competition with the other manufacturers of the day. A report on the apparatus industry in 1983 showed the seven largest producers of the time were: American LaFrance, Emergency One, FMC, Grumman, Mack, Pierce and Seagrave. The second largest producers included companies such as Darley, Hahn, Thibault, Pirsch, and Sutphen. Smaller companies with production under five trucks a month included Boardman, Continental, Farrar, Four-Guys, Luverne, Marion, Middlesex, Sanford, Smeal, Ward, Young and Maxim.

The number of fire apparatus estimated to be in use in the United States was slightly higher than 76,000 pumpers and nearly 7,000 ladder trucks.

In 1985 the production line, with a staff of 38 assembly workers and 12 office employees, was capable of producing as many as 48 trucks per year. Not bad for a small company in tough competition with the larger apparatus manufacturers. The Maxim production process, trucks built from scratch, changed little during this time. Despite not building their own pumps or drive trains, the rest of the vehicles were built from the ground up. They started with two frame channels purchased

This lime-yellow colored chassis, a common look for apparatus in the 1970s, looks like a Ward LaFrance Ambassador for good reason. From 1975 to 1981, Ward LaFrance and Maxim were owned by the same parent company, North Street Associates. Both Ward and Maxim trucks shared similar features and were often built at both plants simultaneously regardless of brand. Pumpers were built in Elmira and aerials were built in Middleboro, regardless of manufacturer.

directly from the steel company. From there, cross members and spring hangers were installed, followed by either the pump or the aerial ladder depending on the type of unit ordered. The engine and body were then installed and the rig painted, tested and delivered. Maxim was only one of five companies left in the United States that custom built their apparatus from scratch. Maxim had prided itself on custom apparatus since day one and they weren't about to change that now. An internal company memo from this era explained the difference between custom and commercial apparatus:

"Custom-built fire trucks must not be confused with commercial fire trucks. A commercial type fire truck is a pump and body put on a commercial truck chassis such as Ford, GMC, Chevrolet, etc. These are low cost, generally mass produced fire truck types sold to government agencies, export sales and small communities with limited budgets. Maxim builds the complete fire truck including chassis, cab, body and aerial ladder, and finishes the entire truck in its Middleboro, Massachusetts plant. Maxim competes in a high-price market, which can be compared to the purchase of Lincoln and Cadillac passenger cars versus Fords and Chevrolets. Maxim is the Cadillac of fire trucks, therefore, desired by municipalities and fire departments that want a custom-built fire apparatus that will last for twenty (20) years and, of great priority, where they can obtain parts for twenty (20) years."

It took roughly 3,000 hours to build an aerial and 1,300 hours to build a pumper. The average cost of a pumper started around $125,000 and the cost of an aerial ladder started around $200,000. Interestingly, municipalities paid for their apparatus on delivery, leaving the company to furnish the costs of materials up front. As a comparison, the costs for the same apparatus, prior to World War II, were - about $8,000 for a pumper and around $18,000 for an aerial ladder. Some of Deane's first apparatus went to Waltham and Swampscott, Massachusetts and Redondo Beach and Costa Mesa, California. Two aerial ladders were delivered to Richmond, Virginia. As owner, president and sole stockholder of Maxim Motor Company, Inc., it was safe to say that David Deane had saved the company from financial ruin for the time being. When reached for comment in 1983, a representative from the Middleborough Trust Company quoted, "When creditors look at the name, they may have difficulty divorcing the new company name from the old. That's got to be the major hurdle." However, the economy and competition were still chipping away at the Maxim mystique. Still overwhelmed by debt, and the slim prospect of the company making a comeback, Deane was not able to hire back all of the 100 employees laid off several years earlier in 1981. Things were going well for Deane, but certain circumstances were out of his control. Deane had hoped to develop a line of heavy-duty aerial ladders to compliment the line of light-duty aerial ladders, however, the company finances were stretched thin

Rear 3/4 view of the truck on the facing page.

and no new investors were willing to take the risks. The economy was just not cooperating. The fire apparatus manufacturing business is one that relies on the spending abilities of its customers—fire departments and municipalities. When economic times are good, orders for new fire apparatus come in faster than they can keep up with. When budgets are stretched, orders are placed on hold and the fire truck companies are at the mercy of the budgets. A search for new investors was not successful and the company was on the road to ruin again.

In 1985, the Maxim firm was closed down again after a foreclosure on the original $900,000 loan. Harley W. (Skip) Waite, owner of Eastern Technologies in Andover, Massachusetts purchased the company, factory, and grounds and reopened it later in 1985 under the name of Maxim Incorporated. He owned several other companies in Massachusetts and Wisconsin that dealt with the manufacture of fuel tankers, re-fuelers, high-tech precision-machined parts and military vehicles. The new ownership with experience in the trucking industry seemed a good match. A positive future was on the horizon once again.

Norton, Massachusetts owned this great looking 1989 F-Model pumper with high side compartments. As fire departments got more specialized, more storage was needed. Most trucks these days utilize any and all available space for storage. *Photo courtesy of Rich Louf*

CHAPTER EIGHT

MODERN YEARS

In October 1986 a shiny new red fire truck rolled out of the doors of the Maxim plant. This truck, an S-Model pumper built for Middleborough Fire Department was, appropriately enough, the last truck built in the Middleboro location. In attempt to improve services and products, Maxim picked up their operations from Wareham Street and moved their facilities to a temporary location at 336 Weir Street in Taunton. This served as an intermediate step towards the final goal of relocating to a brand new building in the Abbey Lane Professional Park in Middleboro. The move from the original building on Wareham Street was expected to increase the efficiency and manufacturing capabilities. The new temporary location in Taunton provided 33,000 square feet of manufacturing and warehouse space, new lighting, machinery centers, and sheet metal fabricating equipment. It was more than sufficient to keep production churning.

The move from Taunton back to Middleboro at 9 Abbey Lane took place in February 1987. The move into the new $3 million dollar building proved promising. The new building contained 60,000 square feet of room and some of the best mechanical and computerized equipment of the time. Some of this equipment included a KWB 60-foot downdraft paint booth, 5-ton bridge cranes, pump and aerial testing facilities, and an impressive inventory of stock. A newsletter supplied by Maxim Incorporated described many of the new additions to the facility that would improve services such as an assembly line production process and CAD computers (Computer Aided Design). However, the fire truck industry was becoming very competitive and some of the large manufacturers were gaining popularity and strength with their new designs and quick turn-around times for new apparatus. Also that year, Harley Waite took on a partner to help with the financial costs of the new facilities. He formed a partnership with Urban Transportation Development Company; a subdivision owned by the Montreal, Canada based Lavelin Corporation Incorporated. The Lavelin Corporation was a worldwide engineering firm and invested over $11 million dollars in the company to improve production and engineering.

Production continued as usual and Maxim kept pace with the changes in the industry now mandated by NFPA standards such as enclosed cabs, aluminum construction, and other safety guidelines. With the new building came new changes to the apparatus designs. The S-Model was no longer available but Maxim did

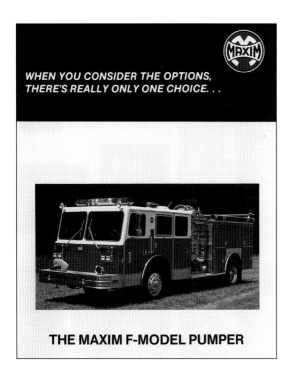

Maxim stayed with the V-front F-Model chassis to keep pace with the other manufacturers who were selling the same styles. This sales brochure, very generic looking on the front, contained 70 pre-engineered options inside and helped a potential customer decide on how to design a vehicle for their communities' needs.

offer two different models of cab forward cabs. The V-cab was more along the lines of the traditional cab forward Maxim customers were used to seeing. This tilt-cab design was manufactured in conjunction with PemFab. The shape changed slightly and it took on the appearance of a more modern looking apparatus with the entire cab becoming more rectangular and the corners becoming squarer with enlarged windshields. According to Maxim literature on the new design:

"The term 'stock' or 'standard' pumper implies a no-frills, stripped-down piece of equipment. It suggests less than adequate components, like cheap axles or insufficient pumps. Unfortunately, in many cases, that is exactly what 'stock' means, and purchasing this type of equipment poses a real threat for municipal security.

The Maxim F-Model pumper is the exception. This is a fully equipped truck, engineered with more safety devices than in any other 'stock' pumper. Safety, performance and reliability are built into the Maxim F-Model pumper. The truck features an extruded aluminum body with a Maxim four-door aluminum cab all sitting on Rockwell axles."

Maxim also offered a Contour cab with a rounded face. It had rounded edges and corners as opposed to the square edges on the traditional F-Model. Some of these Contour cab models went to Marshfield, Massachusetts and the Massachusetts Firefighting Academy in Stow, Massachusetts. The two units that were ordered by the Firefighting Academy were ordered with a unique feature. The pump panels on either side of the pump area were constructed of a clear Lexan material and color-coded plumbing that would allow the new firefighters/recruits to view the inner workings of the pump while it was in operation. This author, during his 11-week recruit training in the summer of 1999, spent quite a bit of time with these trucks. These 11-year-old trucks being used almost every day certainly showed some wear and tear. However, with proper maintenance by the mechanics at the fire academy, the units were in great working shape. With 70 pre-engineered options available, the potential customer had many options in designing apparatus to suit the needs of the community. Delivery time on a new unit was 120 days or less. Maxim also abandoned their custom-made line of aerial ladders and joined forces with RK Manufacturing to produce a new generation of high performance heavy-duty ladders. In August 1989 they began offering these aerial ladders with a 109-foot vertical reach and a 400-pound tip load. Some of the options included a pre-piped master stream, remote monitor, individual outrigger controls and overload alarm.

In 1988, Harley Waite sold his remaining share of ownership to UTDC/Lavelin and they became the sole owner of Maxim Incorporated. One reputable source, a former Maxim employee, reported that when Lavelin took over, they immediately began stockpiling inventory and purchasing a wealth of office supplies. In the process, they cleaned out the office space and threw away many of the old files and sales literature from Maxim's earliest days. An unconfirmed rumor is that a great deal of these original Maxim artifacts and a part of history are now located in a tractor-trailer freight container at the bottom of the Middleboro landfill. Allegedly, pallets upon pallets of literature and manuals were also discarded. Actions like those are truly a fire apparatus collector's nightmare, but business is business. Yet another reputable source reported that most of the original records were not destroyed, but rather shipped back to the main office in Canada. After the building was refurbished, more stock and material began arriving. Items such as axles, transmissions, diesel engines and cabs from the Midwest arrived. Employees reported that it was customary to have a count of two or three of each item laying around for use when needed. But too much stock was ordered and all the while sales continued falling off. The employees could sense trouble brewing.

Several times throughout the late 1980s disagreements between the workers and management turned sour; on several occasions employees held a strike or walked out for various reasons. At issue were union demands for higher pay and better benefits, all the while orders decreased. Union employees belonged to the United Electrical, Radio and Machine Workers of America Local 291. In one case on December 15, 1988, workers held a one-day strike due to a month-long contract dispute and the alleged improper firing of an employee. Workers did return the next day, but more contract lockouts resumed and employees threatened more strikes. Other complications involved legal battles over ladder and chassis designs. Despite rebounding several times and maintaining its reputation for quality products, the orders were just not coming in.

With such a precarious financial situation and ongoing labor problems, UTDC made their desire to sell the company public in October 1989 and President John Mandelli announced that if a buyer wasn't found the plant would close down. Some of the potential buyers that flirted with buying the ailing company included Seagrave Fire Apparatus (who ironically rebounded into one of the top competitors in the 1990s), Emergency One, FMC Corporation, Kovatch, Fire Trucks Ltd and Rosenbauer, along with a long list of private individuals. Some had an interest in business, some were interested in the real estate, and yet others possessed a genuine interest in saving the company. However, none of the prospective buyers chose to risk buying the ailing company in such tough times.

On December 15, 1989, ten days before Christmas, the company closed its doors for good. The floundering state economy once again put undue pressure on the Maxim company to maintain its level of business. With state funding on the decrease and the fact that cities and towns didn't have the money to spend on expensive fire apparatus, fire departments weren't purchasing apparatus as they had before. The stiff competition from the other manufacturers was too much. They consistently underbid Maxim for jobs. Some of the larger companies produced even less than the 45 trucks Maxim did the year before and some giants produced up to 900 trucks a year. The closing left 114 employees out of work for the holiday season and the Lavelin Corporation with an $11 million dollar loss.

On January 10 and 11, 1990, J. C. Tedesco, a company from nearby Hanover that specialized in liquidations and auctions, began auctioning off the land, buildings, office supplies, equipment and tools that belonged to Maxim Incorporated. Some rumors have it that the Maxim company was actually liquidated by the Lavelin Corporation as a tax write-off because the company had become a profit-making organization once again.

Many departments claim to own the last Maxim fire truck ever built—a testament to the reputation of the company. There are a handful of departments that vie for the title and prestige of owning the last Maxim. This is a difficult claim to boast, as there are many factors involved with that decision. There are varying degrees of thought as to which truck was the last Maxim built, and why. The first question pertains to the fact that Maxim nearly went out of business several times before, finally succumbing to the economy. At which time does the department claim to have the last truck? In 1981, 1985 or 1989? In regards to the final closing in 1989, one source has reported that the last serial number assigned was appropriately enough given to a Middleboro fire truck—a 1989 quint. Another source mentions that the very last truck believed to have been built by Maxim was a yellow 1989 F-Model that was delivered to the Affton Fire Protection District in Affton, Missouri and assigned to Engine

Company 1114. This truck was the only truck pictured inside the factory receiving its finishing touches in a feature newspaper article dated December 9, 1989—just days before the factory closed its doors for good. This unit had a 1,250-gpm pump with a 500-gallon booster tank and 30 gallons of foam, and it carried the serial number 30-0012. The sales representative for the area was Leo Ellbracht of Lake St. Louis, Missouri. A neighboring department of Mehlville was also looking for a pair of pumpers to be built, but upon hearing of the financial uncertainties of Maxim, opted to go with a pair of Spartan/FMC pumpers instead. This was, in all probability, the last truck to roll out of the factory doors before they were locked up.

Yet another reliable source, which worked for the Hyannis, Massachusetts fire department at the time of the closing, accompanied the Hyannis Fire Chief to the factory and proceeded to buy a pumper from The Middleborough Trust Company (the bank that took over the assets of the company). Allegedly, this truck was purchased from the bank through a transaction that occurred in the parking lot. No doubt this truck was one of the last finished as the pump plumbing was piped incorrectly, obviously completed in haste before the doors were closed.

When looking at the known facts, there were eight trucks left in the building in late November 1989. Four trucks near completion were: two trucks for the City of New Bedford, a truck for Warren, Rhode Island and the Affton, Missouri rig. There were also three Worcester trucks and an unsold and unfinished stock truck (probably the truck purchased by Hyannis). Other trucks that were built in late 1989 included trucks to Warwick, Rhode Island and Somers, Connecticut. Several original contracts, including the Worcester units,

During the late 1980s Maxim offered two styles of cab forward pumpers, a "V-Front cab" (as seen in the previous two photos) and the "Contour cab," like this pumper from Warwick, Rhode Island. These pumpers could be ordered with four-door enclosed cabs or two-door canopy cabs, with delivery times of less than 120 days. This pumper was one of two identical trucks ordered by the department. *Photo courtesy of Rich Louf*

were canceled when agreements couldn't be reached between City Hall and Maxim. In the case of the Worcester apparatus, the city was still interested in the apparatus, but could not send payment until after January 1—just weeks after the closing and too late to close the deal. This debate over the last Maxim may never be solved and will most likely remain a debatable subject.

Part of the beauty of Maxims is the fact that a great many of them continue to see useful lives and are rehabilitated and re-used by the same department or sent to another department to keep working at what they do best. After being rehabbed, some of these rigs barely show a trace of

the original Maxim that used to remain underneath. Some have been restored to their original and former glory, whether they are pumpers that received new cabs with enclosed jump seats, or a trusty, tired aerial being pulled by a new tractor. The important part is that some of these rigs have received new life. One unit, a 1955 open cab 75-foot aerial from Wareham, Massachusetts was sold to the neighboring community of Marion for $1. The Marion department completed a proper rehab and the truck was placed into service as their first aerial ladder. As of this writing, it's still providing faithful service well into the 21st century—almost 50 years later!

"Craftsmen of the highest caliber who produced trucks regarded for their quality and performance." **Excerpt from "Maxim, An American Tradition," Middleboro-Lakeville Hometown, Bobby Carroll.**

There are also a few stories out there regarding Maxim trucks that were retired from service, bought by private owners and driven many miles to their new homes without incident. One Maxim was purchased from the Dalton, Massachusetts Fire Department in western Massachusetts and driven by its new owner to the state of Maryland in the month of January. The trip was made without any problems. Yet another similar story involves one of the many Maxims purchased by the Indianapolis, Indiana fire department. When they retired a 1964 Maxim S-Model, it was purchased by a firefighter in Palm Beach, Florida who's association with the IFD went back three generations, as his father and great-grandfather were both firefighters in Indianapolis. After buying the rig, the truck was driven

back to Florida some 1,200 miles. Cross-country stories like these prove that these trucks were up to the task and had the stamina to run for extended periods of time under harsh conditions. The unfortunate circumstances are stories of an unconfirmed rumor that the Maxim firm had been approached by a well known trucking firm. This firm had propositioned them and asked the Maxim company to supplement their fire apparatus line by building truck tractors to pull freight trailers, to which Maxim declined. One would have to wonder that if they had agreed to that proposition, would they still be around today? After all, Maxim started out as an automotive company and had twice been successful in the commercial trucking industry. Where have all the Maxims gone?

MAXIM COMPLIMENTS

"Walking through Maxim's plant suggests the mournful eulogies often voiced for Yankee craftsmanship are decidedly premature. It is Yankee craftsmanship welded to top drawer engineering and the best of materials that have won Maxim its good name."
- *New Bedford Standard Times* article dated February 19, 1967

"…this structure was a rambling, cavernous, poorly lighted plant that somehow attracted craftsmen of the highest caliber who produced trucks regarded for their quality and performance."
- *Firefighter's News*, June-July 1987

" If it can be done, Maxim can do it."
- Maxim sales ad, circa 1960s

"…the Maxims turned to an axle supplier for engineering assistance, who agreed to send their best engineer to help work out the required designs. The engineer, C. A. (Bert) Carey arrived in April 1915, and never returned to the axle company."
- Robert Maxim Beals in The Story, "Maxim: Sixty Years, Plus"

"No small part of the success of the company is due to the loyalty of the employees and the pride expressed in their craftsmanship. Some of them remained with the company for half a century or longer."
- History of the Town of Middleboro

"Just a little bit better all around."
- Maxim sales ad, The Fire Engineer, March 1925

"Middleboro's Maxim Motor Company has developed into one of the country's five major builders of fire apparatus with units in operation all over the world."
- *New Bedford Standard Times* article dated July 11, 1954

"Built to last by New England craftsmen who have been building fire apparatus and only fire apparatus through two generations."
- Maxim sales ad, Fire Engineering magazine, June 1946

"There is no more shining exemplification of the success of a small firm than that of the Maxim Motor Company. Because of the exceptional business ability of the owner, Carlton W. Maxim, and pride in their craftsmanship on the part of the employees, the firm grew to be recognized as a leading manufacturer of fire apparatus with a worldwide reputation for the excellence of its product."
- History of the Town of Middleboro

"Over half a century has passed since the first custom-built fire apparatus bearing the Maxim name rolled out of our plant in Middleboro, Massachusetts, beginning a long tradition of proud craftsmanship that has been handed down through three generations…"
- Maxim sales brochure, May 1971

"Custom is our standard. Perfection is our goal. Pride in achievement and product excellence is our way of life. Every Maxim made today is the result of uncompromising integrity. They are built with patience, driven with pride and backed by Maxim… the world's most distinguished name in firefighting apparatus."
- Maxim sales brochure, May 1971

BIBLIOGRAPHY

100 Years of America's Fire Fighting Apparatus, Phil DaCosta, Bonanza Books, New York, 1963

American Fire Engines Since 1900, Walter McCall, Motorbooks International, 1976/1993

American Volunteer Fire Trucks, Donald F. Wood and Wayne Sorensen, Krause Publications, Iola, Wisconsin, 1993

Big City Fire Trucks, Volume I, 1900-1950, Donald F. Wood & Wayne Sorensen, 1996

Big City Fire Trucks, Volume II, 1951-1996, Donald F. Wood & Wayne Sorensen, 1996

Collecting and Restoring Antique Fire Trucks, Robert Lichty, TAB Books, 1981

Fire Engines in North America, Sheila Buff, Wellfleet Press, Secaucus, New Jersey, 1991

Fire Trucks: American Fire Fighters on the Street, Henry Rasmussen, Motorbooks International, Osceola, Wisconsin, 1987

Hiram Percy Maxim, Alice Clink Schumacher, The Ham Radio Publishing Group, 1970

History of the Town of Middleboro 1906-1965, Mertie Romaine

"Maxim, An American Tradition," Middleboro-Lakeville Hometown, Bobbie Carroll, undated newspaper

"Maxim's First Fifty Years", Joseph C. Whitcomb, *The Middleboro Antiquarian, Volume VI, Number 3*, June 1964

Maxim, Sixty Years Plus, Robert Maxim Beals, SPAAMFAA publication

Maxim sales brochures and sales literature, 1914-1989

Maxim Salesmen's scrapbook, 1919-1935 – contains many non-dated newspaper articles, sales literature, sales brochures and other miscellaneous artifacts pertaining to the company

Maxim Trucks, Herman Sass, self-published, Buffalo, New York, 1996

Sanford Fire Apparatus: An Illustrated History, Joe Raymond Jr., Engine House Publishers, 1986

Some Smaller North East Fire Apparatus Manufacturers, Don Mason, undated, private publication

The American Fire Engine, Hans Halberstadt, Motorbooks International, 1993

"The Horseless Carriage Comes to Middleboro", *The Middleboro Antiquarian, Volume 5, Number 2*, April 1963

The Rise of an American Inventor: Hudson Maxim's Life Story, Clifton Johnson, Doubleday, Page & Company, 1927

"Under Fire, An Old New England Industry Retrenches as Municipal Budgets Shrink," *New England Business Magazine*, January 1991

"U.S. Army Trucks at War", *War Department Technical Manual TM5-687*, Inspection and Preventive Maintenance Services for Fire Protection Equipment and Appliances, January 1946

Ward LaFrance Fire Trucks 1918-1978 Photo Archive, John J. Burzichelli & Richard J. Gergel, Iconografix Photo Archive Series, 2000

INDEX

INDEX